AUSTRALIAN NATIVE GARDENING – MADE EASY

AUSTRALIAN NATIVE GARDENING – MADE EASY

DICK CHADWICK

LITTLE HILLS PRESS

Acknowledgements

Many people helped and encouraged me in the preparation of this book. I am grateful to them all. Special thanks are due to the following:

General

My wife Janet and children (Rick, Louise & Peter) for their help, support and encouragement.
Margot & Norman Davies, Pat Pritchard & Melda Oswald all of Hawkes Nest, N.S.W., Peta & Gavin Carrick of Forestville, N.S.W., and Margaret & Terry Livermore of Killarney Heights, N.S.W.

Technical

Without the advice and assistance of David Ratcliffe of Raymond Terrace, N.S.W., my task would have been much more onerous and less enjoyable and the results not nearly as successful.
My thanks go also to his wife, Pat, for her patience.
The excellent drawings and graphics were prepared by my long-time friend, Bill O'Donnell of Forestville, N.S.W.

Manuscript

Julie Holton performed numerous small miracles in producing the manuscript. I am very grateful for and appreciative of her excellent work.

Photographs

Many of the photographs used in this book were loaned by the Newcastle branch of the Society for Growing Australian Plants from their Charles Shipway Library. Bev and Geoff Rigby were most helpful in assisting me to make selections. Mr. Shipway kindly gave his consent to the use of library photographs taken by him, and these are indicated by his initials 'C.H.S.'. Others who took library photographs used are Dr. Paddy Lightfoot & Dr. Gordon Cousins; and I thank them all.

Mervyn Hodge of Queensland – a well known SGAP member – was a very significant source of high quality photographs. The time and effort he expended in assisting me were exceptional, and I am very grateful to him. Merv's photographs are indicated by his initials 'M.W.H.'.

David Ratcliffe and I took many photographs on a number of joint expeditions. Sid Reynolds kindly allowed us extensive access to his excellent nursery and garden, as did Stan and Marguerite Parkes, whose 2 acre native garden is a real joy to behold.

Dick Chadwick,
Forestville, N.S.W.,

First published in paperback in 1987
Published 1985, reprinted 1986, 1989, 1997, 1999, 2000
Little Hills Press,
37 Alexander Street,
Crows Nest, 2065 N.S.W. Australia

© Dick Chadwick 1985
Designed by Pam Brewster and Nick Charalambous
Typeset by Deblaere Typesetting Pty. Ltd.
Printed by Kyodo Printing Co (S'pore) Pte Ltd

Chadwick, Dick.
    Australian native gardening made easy.
    1st pbk. ed.
    Bibliography.
    Includes index.
    ISBN 0 949773 54 9.

    1. Wild flower gardening – Australia. 2. Gardening – Australia. I. Title.
635.9'676'0994

CONTENTS

FOREWORD

(From Me to You)

This book is intended for the people who are new to Australian Native Gardens, or who have been delighted by the colour photographs of our many beautiful native plants in a book but have been confused by the seemingly complex texts.

Gardening should be — and is — fun. It should be — and is — simple to establish and maintain a first rate garden of Australian Natives.

A bit of heavy work may be required in initial preparation. Subsequently, all that's needed in a properly made native garden is an occasional stroll to keep an eye on things and enjoy the results of your hard work.

All my life I've enjoyed the marvellous variety and beauty of the Australian bush. If this book encourages you to begin and achieve your own native garden, I'll be well rewarded.

Happy Gardening!

Dick Chadwick.

INTRODUCTION

Are Australian Natives easy to grow?

There are several thousand different plants native to Australia. As one would expect in such a large country, with such diverse climatic conditions, there are plants to suit every circumstance — from desert to alpine regions.

But — back to the question — are they easy to grow? The short answer is 'Yes'. However, a more correct answer is 'Yes — providing the correct plant is chosen for the particular circumstance'.

Now, this doesn't mean you have to be a genius to make a selection. It *does* mean you have to observe, apply commonsense and make use of the advice given in this book and other competent sources.

If you do these things, growing Australian Natives *is* easy. They are easy to plant, easy in their water requirements, and easy to look after.

What about maintenance?

If you're game to go the whole way, there's not much to do. Half an hour each weekend is more than enough, even for a large garden.

Once or twice a year you may apply fertilizer — but you don't have to. You may prune occasionally — but again, you don't have to.

A few minutes each *month* will attend to weeds. You may have to squash the odd grub, prune a broken branch, or pick up some of the larger sticks which fall from your trees.

You don't want it so easy?

If you get hooked, there's plenty to do. You can specialise in various species of plants; add a native pool; grow ferns; or get into propagation from seeds and cuttings and/or grafting.

So don't worry if you're a 'gardenaholic'. You can make work — and enjoyable and rewarding work at that — without any trouble at all.

The 6 'P''s (Well, nearly)

These are:

1. Planning
2. Preselection
3. Preparation
4. Purchasing
5. Planting
6. Maintenance

Each of these steps is critical. If you're quick, you'll have noticed, that 'Maintenance' doesn't start with P — but I couldn't think of a better word that does and 'M' is pretty close anyway.

You'll notice that the second 'P' is 'Preselection'. Why 'Preselection'? What happens is you'll pick your plants from the lists and photographs given later, but some you won't be able to buy when you want to.

At this stage, the urge to 'go' is strong! Unless your tolerance level is very high, you'll just have to get something else to fill that spot.

Alternatively, you'll see a beautiful offering at your favourite nursery and will change your mind.

In either case, if you've got your PLANNING & PRESELECTION

right, you'll know the *type* of plant you want, and you won't make a fatal mistake.

The other headings should be self-explanatory. But don't worry — I'll explain them in detail later on.

Names

Sorry about this — but all plants in this book are given their botanical names. And, believe it or not, they're not all so hard. For instance 'Eucalyptus' and 'Grevillea' are botanical names, and I'll bet you've heard of both.

The names are not hard to learn — they are a bit like phone numbers. If you try, you'll get it. Unless your spouse (or friend) is involved, they will think you're learning a foreign language at first (as you will be — it's mostly Latin and Greek) but think how proud you'll be when you can 'drop' botanical names to that friend who's won the last three local garden competitions in a row — particularly if he doesn't understand you!

Seriously though, the only way to properly identify a plant is to use its botanical name. Different common names are applied to the same plant in various parts of the country, but the botanical name will be the same.

To ease the pain, I've included some popular common names. You can use these when you talk to the uninitiated.

Don't forget — it's better to mispronounce a botanical name than to buy the wrong plant!

Other topics

The separate chapter on Grevilleas might be a surprise. There are more than 270 recognised species of Grevillea, and what a wondrous assortment they are!

I haven't seen a native garden without a Grevillea, and their popularity, hardiness, diversity and beauty are such that I felt they deserved a chapter of their own. (After all, it is my book!)

If you are (or become) interested in natives, you'll very likely be keen to attract some of our gorgeous native birds to your garden. So, there's a special chapter about birds — how to attract them and provide for their needs.

Finally, there's a short chapter ('If now you're hooked...') which will be helpful if you want to become a real expert — or even if you'd like to become a little more involved.

The plants

464 plants are described and their characteristics are tabulated in a way which is easily understood (promise!).

Recommendations are made for all conditions likely to be encountered in the average garden.

The plants listed are commercially available, and if you're prepared to look around you'll be able to buy them. As you'll see, alternative approaches are suggested in case you get stuck.

Now to the serious stuff!!

PLANNING YOUR GARDEN

Why plan?

Even a simple holiday is usually preceded by quite a lot of planning — particularly if you have children to consider. An overseas trip is likely to take months or even years of discussion and negotiation before arrangements are complete.

In these instances, you're trying to ensure that you'll have a happy and enjoyable time. But bear in mind that such holidays are of comparatively short duration — even though the memories may linger forever.

Your garden will impact on your life every day. If you work, you'll see it every day as you prepare for and leave for the slave mines and again when you return. If you're into homemaking, you'll be in and out of the garden most days. Of course, at the weekends, the whole family will spend time outside the house.

The message is that your garden is very important to you — emotionally and physically. And, if you've bought this book, it's more important to you than to most people. So it's worth taking a lot of trouble to get it right. This requires PLANNING.

PLANNING takes time and effort. But your basic planning is a 'once-off' exercise. The time you spend in this phase will be both enjoyable and well rewarded in the future.

What can we expect from a garden?

The main things we can look to our garden to provide are:-
1. Aesthetic appeal
2. Privacy
3. Recreation
4. Protection from the elements
5. Minimum maintenance

Aesthetic appeal

Well done, your garden will be a thing of beauty. It should complement the house, so that the whole setting has a feeling of integration.

Natives can provide the colours, textures and forms to satisfy all requirements. They can be used to hide ugly services, soften harsh outlines and eliminate disturbing views.

Your garden design must have as a major objective the achievement of harmony with the site and house — all elements should blend together. Beauty, of course, is in the eye of the beholder. What appeals to you might not appeal to me. But that's one of the great things about a garden — it's a medium through which you can express yourself with very little outside interference. Even this usually involves only proper consideration of your neighbours.

Privacy

Proper planting will give visual privacy and can help reduce (or contain) noise. As mentioned earlier, you can 'plant out' unwanted views, and substitute your own vistas.

Generally speaking, you won't want your neighbours to see into your house — and vice versa. Heavy screen planting is not always necessary to achieve this — all that's needed is enough to break up the view. And bear in mind that if you achieve this, you'll be able to keep open your curtains all the time — or dispense with them altogether.

Max Hewitt's garden at Mt Kuringai, N.S.W.

Heavy planting is necessary to reduce noise substantially, but you can achieve an acoustic screen which is a good sound absorber.

Removing unwanted views can be easy. At one time we were confronted with the back of a new house. It wasn't particularly attractive, and neither of us had much privacy in our gardens. Two quick growing wattles solved the problem promptly and effectively and gave us a great outlook in that direction.

A sense of solitude and peace can be achieved in the busiest suburb on the smallest piece of land. This may be critical if you want to spend a lot of time in your garden and want to entertain friends without neighbourly involvement.

Recreation

A major consideration is young children. If you don't have any (or don't intend to) a lawn is completely unnecessary. I haven't had one for years, and one of my great moments occurred when I gave away my lawnmower, edge trimmer and clippers. I admit my children were in their teens at the time.

If you do have young children, plan a family or have a well-loved dog, a lawn may be important. On the other hand, a suitably paved area may be very satisfactory for their needs.

Bear in mind that a lawn is time consuming and very demanding. You may well be better off without it. In any case, it's easy to convert a native garden to lawn if your needs change.

Probably you'll want a barbecue, and an area for having meals outside with family and friends. You may have a pool, or wish to install one later, in which case you will have to plant the future pool area appropriately.

Your garden should be a place in which you can relax and enjoy yourself — on your own or with others. Don't be a slave to it — it shouldn't tie you down or worry you.

Protection from the elements

Besides protecting your privacy from the outside world, your garden can provide protection against sun and wind.

Sun control through the use of appropriate plants is usually neglected — but it's a very effective and economical way to handle it.

In Australia, summer sun should be kept off North, East and West walls. Trees and shrubs can do this job for you, and at the same time will cool the air around the house as a result of moisture being breathed out through their leaves. Judicious planting will allow northern winter sun to enter the house and provide no-cost heating just when it's needed.

Screen planting to protect your garden from unpleasant prevailing winds can be a necessity if you wish to establish your garden satisfactorily. This applies especially near the sea, where strong salt laden winds at all times of the year are a real problem. But plants are available which thrive on these conditions and even grow rapidly. You can plant these as a temporary measure to provide shelter for your young plants until they get established — then remove the temporary screen plants.

In essence, you can do a lot to create your own 'micro climate'. But you won't do it in a few weeks — it may take from two to five years to get a good result, particularly if you're starting with a bare block.

Minimum maintenance

Routine maintenance in many gardens is an ever demanding chore. Even if you're a keen gardener, surely it's better to spend your time in constructive and rewarding activities (such as planting new flowers or propagating your own plants) rather than mowing, doing edges and so on.

A properly prepared native garden will give you loads of spare time. After the intitial effort, input will be largely up to you. Demands on your time will be minimal, and you can spend your extra leisure any way you like — and this may well include improving your garden or your knowledge of natives.

The plan

BEFORE you put pencil to paper, go and look at some gardens. Your viewing can be as restricted as strolling around your own suburb, or as extensive as visiting botanical gardens. Visit a few nurseries in your area — they usually have their own landscaping, and naturally try to show their plants to their best advantage.

The object of this is to find out what you like — and what you don't. Most people who have good gardens are only too happy to help a beginner, and 'show off' their own garden at the same time. Usually, you'll get good advice and it's both free and sincere. And, who knows, you might make some new friends. But be selective in the advice you take — it won't *all* be good.

Make notes of your visits — names, addresses and phone numbers — and, in particular, note the names of any plants (including trees) which appeal to you. One of the advantages of this approach is that you'll soon discover which plants grow well in your area, and any special treatment they'll need.

Now, put your property on paper. If you're not much good at drawing, use graph paper. A good scale is 1 in a hundred — i.e., 10 mm equals 1 metre. Don't overlook the original plans of the house which will make life easy if they're available.

Things you must include on your plan are:–
· Sewer lines and septic tank
· Overhead wires
· Paths and access tracks (to electrical switchboard, gas or electric meters, garden shed, pool filter etc.)
· Significant natural features e.g., large rocks, rock shelves, hills & hollows
· Existing trees & shrubs you wish to retain
· Swimming pool
· Clothes line/drying area

An inexpensive 30 metre cloth measuring tape will be useful to get measurements — although you don't need to locate things to a very high degree of accuracy.

Don't put anything *proposed* on this original plan. Buy some tissue paper (often called 'butter paper' by draughtsmen) and a soft (say 2B) pencil. Lay this transparent paper over your plan and start sketching in what you'd like. Alternatively, you can sketch on photocopies. Examples of possible treatments are shown on the following pages.

Try and produce a few different schemes. Each must show (assuming you want them):–
· outdoor entertainment area (including barbecue)
· play area (s)

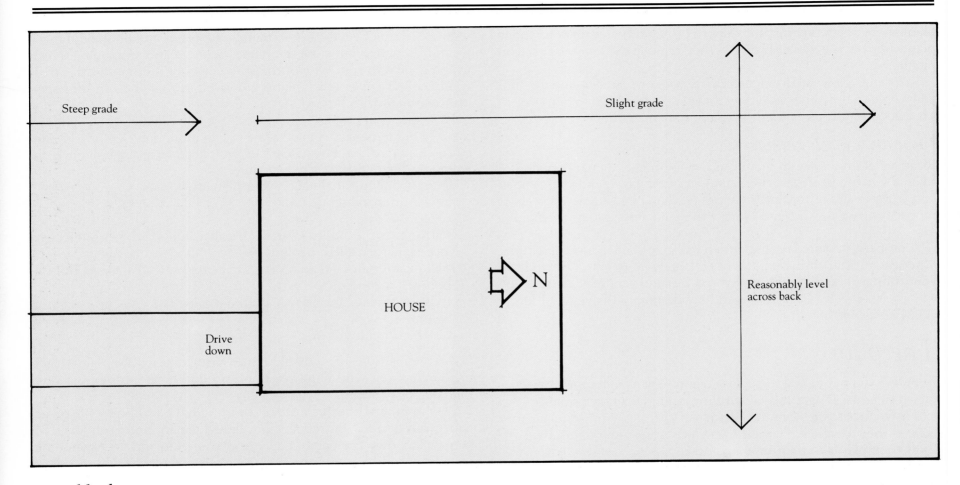

Bare block

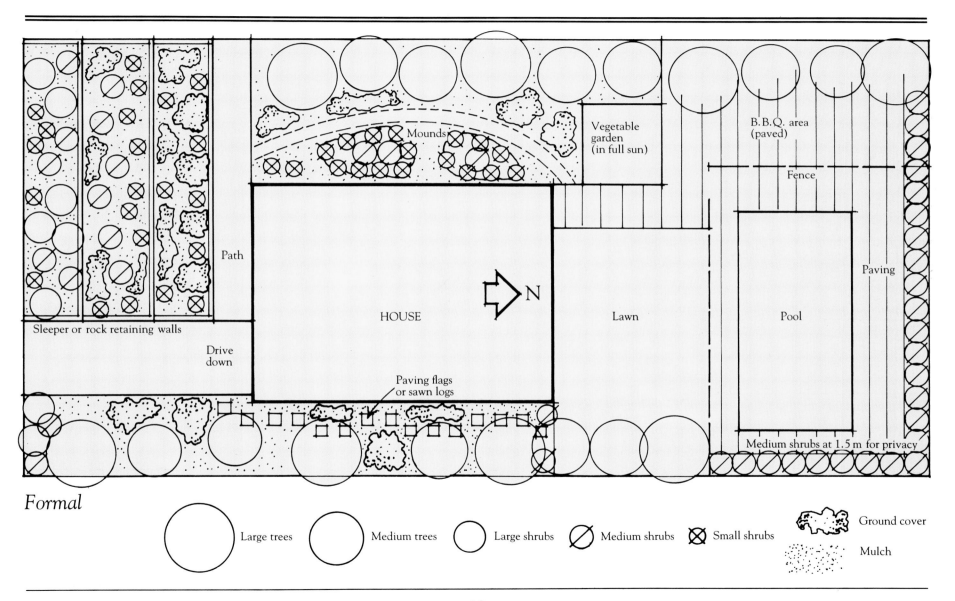

Mounds

Vegetable
garden
(in full sun)

B.B.Q. area
(paved)

Fence

Path

Paving

Sleeper or rock retaining walls

HOUSE

N

Lawn

Pool

Drive
down

Paving flags
or sawn logs

Medium shrubs at 1.5 m for privacy

Formal

Large trees

Medium trees

Large shrubs

Medium shrubs

Small shrubs

Ground cover

Mulch

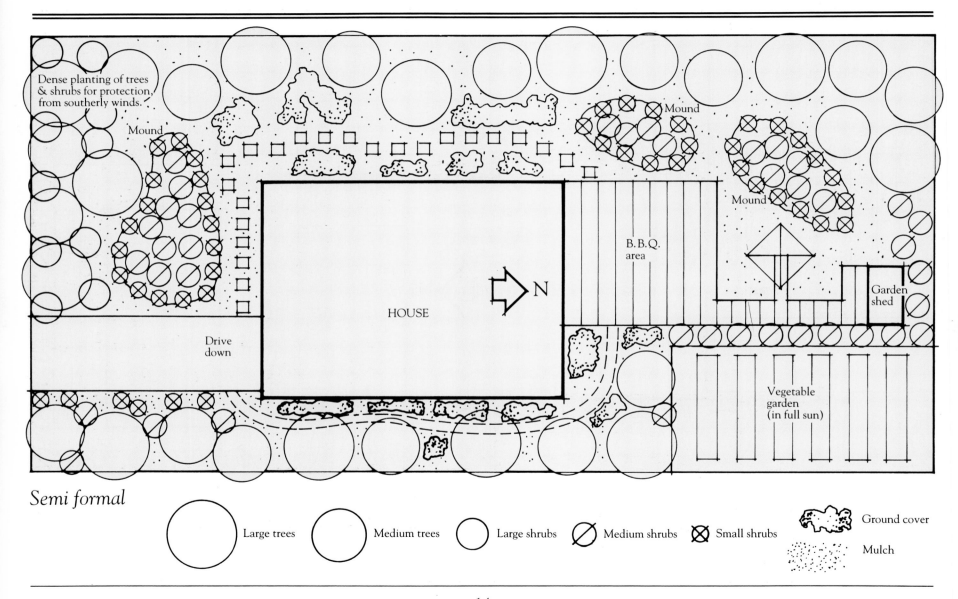

Dense planting of trees & shrubs for protection from southerly winds.

Mound

Mound

Mound

HOUSE

N

Drive down

B.B.Q. area

Garden shed

Vegetable garden (in full sun)

Semi formal

Large trees   Medium trees   Large shrubs   Medium shrubs   Small shrubs

Ground cover

Mulch

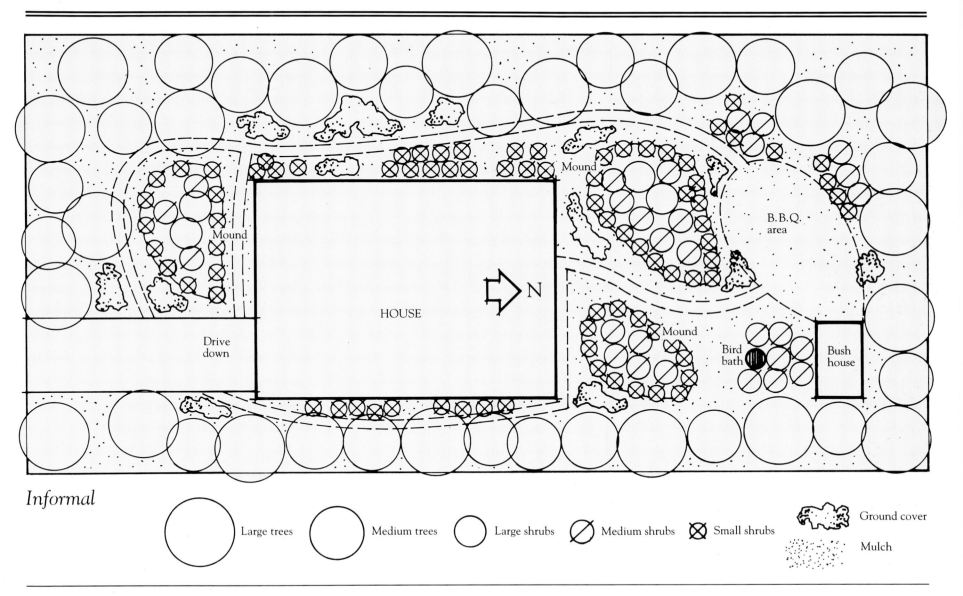

Informal

HOUSE

Drive
down

Mound

Mound

Mound

B.B.Q.
area

Bird
bath

Bush
house

N

Large trees

Medium trees

Large shrubs

Medium shrubs

Small shrubs

Ground cover

Mulch

You *may* wish to include:–
· vegetable and/or herb garden
· shaded area for ferns
· storage area for garden equipment, compost etc
· future swimming pool
· water feature (pool or waterfall)
· rockery

Do not try to retain trees or shrubs which are staggly or diseased, or drastically interfere with your plan. And, if you're in a new or near new house, don't rely too heavily on existing trees, as they may well die as a result of interference with their habitat resulting from building operations.

Don't be concerned about removing existing paths — they are

Marguerite Parks' garden at Bolwarra, N.S.W.

easily and economically replaced, particularly in a native garden. Paths in an informal native garden can be mulch (see later), gravel, brick or stone paving or sawn sections of logs.

Bear in mind that you have a number of basic choices. These are:–

1. All Native Garden

This may be
· Formal
· Informal
· Jungle

2. Mixture of Native & Traditional Gardens

In this case, the Native section may be treated in any of the three ways listed above.

It's all up to you — it's your garden, and you can please yourself.

However, I'm going to proceed on the basis that you want an informal native garden. Formal gardens incorporating natives are too stiff for my liking. 'Jungle' native gardens tend to become a mess, quickly become hard to look after and tend to limit your access to the garden.

My definition of an informal garden is one in which you can walk around, check each plant without difficulty, and gain ready access to any part of your garden.

Once you've made your decisions, you're ready for the next step — Preselection. Don't worry about selecting plants just yet — but continue to spend some time reading about the plants in this book, and visiting gardens and nurseries.

Now, if the steps set out in this chapter are beyond you, don't be embarrassed. You're probably good at something else; maybe you can play the violin, or fly a plane. You may need help from a landscape designer. If you do use one, ask first what a design will cost and the names of customers with whom you can check before you make a commitment. However, a good landscape designer can be an excellent investment.

PRESELECTION OF PLANTS

In the planning process, you will have determined in general terms where and what you want in the way of ground covers and shrubs and trees of various size. Inspections of gardens and nurseries will have produced a partial list of plants you like.

Now is the time to complete your list.

Refer to 'The Plants' chapter. It is divided into two parts:

Characteristics at a Glance and

Descriptions

The table, 'Characteristics at a Glance', will simplify the selection process. You will become familiar with the meaning of the symbols quite quickly, and they will guide you to those plants which meet your specific requirements.

In 'Descriptions', each plant listed is described briefly and any particular features or requirements are noted. In most cases, a colour photograph accompanies the description. Together, the description and picture will help you to visualize the plant and how it might contribute to your garden.

To further assist you, plants are in alphabetical order (by botanical name), and each one is numbered. The same number is used throughout the book.

Ensure that you use the table and the descriptions together, so that you can quickly discard plants which are unsuitable for one reason or another. For instance, you may want a small shrub near a path, but you find from the description that it is 'prickly', and this might be a nuisance to people who might brush against it.

There are more than 20,000 plants native to Australia. However, many are not grown commercially, some are unsuitable for the home

Melaleuca fulgens (salmon form)

garden (for a number of reasons) and some are difficult to grow and maintain.

All the plants listed are grown commercially, and are pretty easy to grow providing conditions are reasonable. The few exceptions are noted. With some searching, you should be able to locate the great majority of those listed, and your problems with them will be minimal.

So, get your list together, realising it is unlikely it will be final. You will change your mind, and there may be some plants you cannot buy. You'll be looking around for some weeks yet while you carry out the next step — Preparation.

PREPARATION FOR PLANTING

As with Planning, proper preparation is critical for real success. Poor preparation will result in poor growth, dead plants, and — worst of all — a lot more maintenance than is necessary.

The time and effort you spend now will be repaid a hundredfold in the future so — DO IT RIGHT!

You should appreciate that this is the *only* part of establishing your garden that requires some hard physical work. That's the bad news. The good news is that it will get you fit (or keep you that way), and you'll get a great deal of satisfaction out of a job well done and the knowledge that a few days effort now will be amply rewarded. And, it's not nearly as hard as it might appear at first sight — you will get worthwhile and noticeable results right from the start.

Now to the nitty-gritty:

You will be faced with one of the following situations (or a combination of them):

· An established traditional garden (perhaps with lawns, flowers, shrubs etc) which you want to change.
· A mess — weeds rubbish etc.
· Comparatively untouched native bush.

In each case, your basic approach will be the same.

Step 1: Get rid of all the 'rubbish'.

Definition: 'Rubbish' in this context means *everything* you don't want in your new garden. It may include lawn, shrubs, flowers — and even trees.

Be tough! Don't keep shrubs and trees you don't want because they *are* shrubs and trees or they are 'living things'. This is especially so if such plants are sick, straggly or otherwise badly shaped, or you just don't like them. They may be causing unwanted shade, or blocking views.

So make your decisions, and carry them out expeditiously. You'll be amazed how good you feel.

Bear in mind that if you wish to remove large trees, you may have to obtain approval from your local council, and you'll need to have good reasons. Generally, if you intend to replant, you won't have much trouble. Also your tree(s) may be big enough to warrant the attention of a professional (but get three or four quotations before you proceed, because this can be expensive).

The only completely satisfactory way to get rid of living things in your garden is to dig them out. In particular, this applies to weeds. And don't just pull or chop off the tops. Dig, and get rid of everything. And do it thoroughly — don't miss little ones, because they do grow up.

Generally, I'm against the use of weedkillers. But if you do have weeds you can't eradicate with reasonable effort, seek professional advice. Make sure you stipulate that you don't wish to poison the soil. Use weedkiller very carefully, and strictly in accordance with the manufacturer's instructions, with particular emphasis on aspects relating to the safety of you and your family.

Step 2: Prepare the soil

Now that you've removed all unwanted material — including weeds — you can move into the next phase. Incidentally, preparing the soil as described in this step will ensure that you will get rid of most of the unwanted growth you may have missed in Step 1.

The important part of the soil is the top 300 mm (12 inches) or so. This is to be thoroughly broken up and aerated. If your soil is already a friable (crumbly) type, you only have to go over it thoroughly with a large garden fork. If it's too hard for this, loosen it up with a mattock first, *then* go over it thoroughly with a fork.

Then rake the surface thoroughly with a steel rake.

This process will (quite literally) turn up all the weeds and roots you missed first time around.

If you have to dig around natives which you wish to retain, be careful. Many have roots close to the surface and they don't appreciate too much disturbance. On the other hand, many species are pretty tough, and will withstand a reasonable amount of rough treatment.

Generally speaking, natives require an open, well drained soil. As most of Australia has this type of soil, this is usually not a problem.

However, if your soil is very heavy, it should be 'loosened up' by the addition of 150 mm (6 inches) of river sand which is mixed thoroughly (with spade or fork) with the top 300 mm (12 inches) of soil. Of course, this will result in 150 mm (6 inches) more material in your planting area than that with which you started. If this extra material is a problem, you can use it for mounds or raised beds, both of which are beneficial for drainage and add interest to the garden.

Raised beds and mounds make for excellent drainage and encourage deep rooting. Done in free-form styles, they can look very natural and attractive. They will also allow you to grow plants which may otherwise be difficult. They may be the answer where the ground is difficult to prepare as previously suggested.

If the soil is clayey, often it can be broken up by the addition of about 1½ kg of Gypsum per square metre. The powdered Gypsum must be thoroughly mixed with the top 300 mm (12 inches) of soil.

Note that if the tasks outlined in Steps 1 & 2 seem daunting because of the size of your garden, you will find they appear easier if you break the garden up into manageable areas. Once an area is done, it is comparatively easy to keep it weed free until you're ready for Step 3. But steps 1 & 2 must be complete before Step 3 unless you have sections of garden quite independent of one another — in which case you can complete all steps in one section at a time.

Step 3: Forming the soil and drainage

Put on your beret and smock — this is an artistic effort!

You are now going to shape your friable soil into its final form. Because it has all been thoroughly broken up, it will be easy to move and shape — all you may need is a shovel and rake. If large quantities of material are to be moved long distances, a wheelbarrow will be a necessity.

Shape your garden the way you planned it. Make sure you get a slope (1 in 100 is minimum) on all surfaces to assist surface run off in heavy rain.

Now is the time to install subsoil drainage if you have a real drainage problem. Perforated plastic pipe is cheap and effective for this purpose. If you don't know how to go about this you should seek advice — you're sure to have a friend or neighbour who can help. The variety of conditions which can arise is infinite, and only an inspection of your particular garden will indicate the solution. However, if water drains away quickly in heavy rain, you probably won't need any special drainage.

It's also now time to place those bush rocks and logs you may wish to use to add interest. Whatever you do, place them in a natural position e.g., flat rocks should be laid flat — not on edge.

Wherever your soil abuts a path or wall, finish the surface of the soil 100 mm (4 inches) below the top of the path or where you want the finished garden level to meet the wall. This allows for 'mulching' (see Step 6) which will make up the difference. For the same reason, don't bury rocks deeply in the soil — just bed them firmly, as you want some depth around them to allow for mulch. Just place the logs on the soil surface. When mulch is applied they can be lifted and the mulch applied under them.

Bear in mind that in carrying out your sculpture, you may remove much or all of your 300 mm (12 inches) of prepared soil from a particular area. If this is the case, you have to prepare the newly exposed ground in this area in the same way as previously described.

Step 4: Have a rest

You'll like this — particularly if you're allergic to physical activity.

Do nothing for 4-6 weeks.

If you're bored, keep reading the book, look at more gardens, and visit nurseries. Maybe you can start to hone in on supply sources for mulch and plants.

But leave the garden alone — just watch the weeds grow (and they will!).

Step 5: What, more digging?

This is the second last step before planting.

Take your trusty garden fork, and thoroughly dig over the whole area again. Carefully remove all weeds. Rake level to your already established contours.

This is pretty easy, as the already prepared soil is very easy to dig, and the weeds are thus simple to remove.

The purpose of this activity is to eliminate any weeds you missed last time around. The delay of 4-6 weeks will allow most of the weed seeds in the soil a chance to germinate, so that you can remove the young unwanted invaders.

Step 6: This is it!

The next step is mulching.

What is mulch? Mulch is a layer of organic or inorganic material which is pervious to water and whose purpose is to keep moisture in the soil and minimise weed growth. If you go for a walk in the bush, you'll notice leaf litter everywhere, and no weeds. Sometimes the litter is quite thick — 150 mm (6 inches) or more. If you lift it up, you'll find it's cool and moist underneath it. This is the effect we want to produce in your garden.

Some experienced gardeners and experts will argue that mulching should be done after planting, and they won't like my approach. But, as I've said before, this is my book, and what I'm recommending is the way I've done it for years — and it works.

Garden newly mulched with pine bark.   Author's garden at Forestville, N.S.W.

Mulched garden   Botanical gardens, Canberra, A.C.T.

Luckily there are several other materials which are satisfactory for mulches. The two I recommend are chipped pine bark (*not* pine chips) and hardwood (eucalypt) chips. Both are available in most areas, are relatively inexpensive, and weather quickly to a pleasant colour.

Other excellent mulches (such as almond or macadamia husks) may be available as a result of a local industry — but they're not generally available. However, if they are, by all means use them.

River gravel — up to 200 mm or ¾ inch diameter — is excellent and attractive; crushed marble chips and broken tile are also used. However, all these are noisy to walk on (which may be an advantage if you're worried about intruders), look untidy when natural litter begins to form, and, as they get older (5 years or so) become difficult to maintain.

So, I'll assume you'll use pine bark or hardwood chips (although much the same principles apply to all mulches).

Recommended depth is 75-100 mm (3-4 inches). In calculating requirements, work on 100 mm (4 inches) — it's better to have too much than too little. Then, work out the area to be covered in square metres, and divide by 10. The answer is the number of cubic metres you need. For example, if the area is $120\,m^2$, you need 12 cubic metres. (1 cubic metre is equal to about 1.3 cubic yards.)

When you have the mulch delivered, buy in bulk (see 'Purchasing'), and try to have it tipped on a smooth, hard surface near the job — a concrete driveway is ideal, but a few sheets of hardboard laid on the ground will suffice. While these mulches are light, they are much easier to shovel from the bottom than the top — you need a surface under the mulch to keep it clean and slide your shovel on.

Do not use a plastic underlay. This is not optional — it's a bad and unnecessary practice. People think that it stops weed growth. It does, but so does the mulch. Most — if not all — weeds which appear after mulching (and these won't be many) result from wind blown seed

The reasons for mulching now are simple. First, you've eliminated the weeds. If you don't thoroughly mulch the surface now, more will germinate and grow. Second, once you've carried out your mulching, your garden will be clean and you can walk around on it without fear of carrying dirt into the house on your shoes. Finally, you're about to start planting. It will take quite a while — weeks or months — to get everything you want and plant it. If you mulch first, moisture will be retained in the soil over the whole area and the plants' roots will be protected from day one.

Natural leaf litter is the best mulch of all, but is rarely available.

which germinates in the mulch itself. Plastic sheet won't stop this. What the plastic does do is completely foul up even distribution of moisture from the surface, and concentrate it around the stems of your plants. It also causes excessive run off, and on steep slopes can cause the mulch to wash off. So — don't use it.

Laying the mulch itself has to be done quite carefully for optimum results. The objective is to ensure that you get uniform cover and not get soil mixed in with the mulch.

This means that you should work in small sections at a time, and place the mulch by hand. Don't just shovel it all over the place — you won't get uniform thickness that way.

An ordinary housebrick laid on edge is about 110 mm (4.5 inches) high. Bricks are ideal for gauging mulch depth. You'll need about a dozen for the job.

Besides the bricks, you'll need a couple of large baskets (the plastic ones used by fish shops are good) and a pneumatic tyred wheelbarrow.

Bear in mind that your garden is bare soil, carefully raked to contours. You don't want to tramp all over it leaving big holes in your wake, or ruin it with barrow wheel marks. So, fill your container and/or barrow with mulch. Start at the edge of your garden nearest to the mulch pile. Lay out your bricks on edge in a random pattern (but roughly circular) in the area you propose to cover. Put the bricks on edge, of course, about 300-500 mm (12-20 inches) apart. *Carefully,* tip the mulch between the bricks, and spread it out so that it is reasonably level and about 10 mm (½ inch) below the top of the bricks.

Your intention is to create a mulch 'working platform' from which you can radiate to the rest of the garden area. So, remove the bricks, place them in the next area to be done, fill in the holes they've left, and go on to the next area.

It's surprising how effectively the mulch you've laid spreads the load from your feet and the barrow. However, keep away from an unsupported mulch edge (i.e., the mulch 'front') or it will slip and the mulch will get mixed in with the soil.

All this sounds a bit fussy, but it's quite simple and doesn't take long. As an example, a friend and I recently placed 20 cubic metres (i.e., a semi-trailer load) of hardwood chip mulch on a steeply sloping garden in 6 hours — but we did work hard. On the other hand, he'd never done it before, and I'm a comparative amateur.

Continue until the whole area is covered, taking particular care to get 'clean' (i.e., soil-free) junctions with paths, walls, rocks etc. If necessary, sweep away soil on vertical surfaces with a small broom before you place the mulch against them.

Your garden will be bare, but it will now be neat and clean. Give it a good watering (soaker hose or sprinkler) for a couple of hours. This will settle the dust and moisten the soil underneath.

You can now plant at your leisure, knowing that your garden is receptive, plants will be protected from the moment they're in place, and you have out-manoeuvred the weeds.

As your plants grow — particularly the trees — they will drop leaves and twigs which will form a natural mulch — the best and most attractive of all. This will happen a lot sooner than you might think, and quite quickly your garden will lose its initial artificial 'new' look.

The Fourth 'P'

PURCHASING

Make sure you read this chapter before you buy *anything*. The advice given is intended to help you get good value for money — and this means good quality at an economic price.

The biggest savings you will make will result from buying in bulk — whether it's soil or sand, mulch or plants. Significant money savings are available, but you'll also save a lot of time, phone calls and petrol if you 'get organised' and do things properly.

It's quite likely that supplies of sand/soil and mulch will come from two different suppliers. Plants are likely to come from a number of suppliers, but the majority of your purchases will come from one or two.

How does one locate suitable suppliers? Sources are many, but here are a few of the best:
- Check your *local* newspaper
- Check your *regional* newspaper
- Check local and regional trade directories
- Check the yellow pages of your telephone directory
- Ask friends and neighbours who have already been through the process.

A glance at the classified ads in your regional newpaper will soon alert you to the savings possible from buying sand/soil and mulch in bulk. For example, buying pine bark in bags as opposed to truckloads could mean that you'll pay *several times* what's necessary. And, of course, different suppliers will have different prices anyway.

So, before you set out looking for prices and suppliers, work out exactly the quantity you need. Do everything you can to buy this quantity in one purchase. That way you'll get the best price and you'll

Anigozanthos humilis

get the job done faster, if for no other reason than that having the material available will encourage you to place (or plant) it just to get it out of the way.

If your block has difficult access, you may be tempted to do a little at a time. But it's probable that, with some thought, you'll find that you can make space available for bulk deliveries.

Now, here are a few tips. When buying sand/soil or mulch, it's ideal if you can have it tipped on a concrete or bitumen drive. You'll find it is much easier to shovel and keep clean. If you can't do this, try using large sheets of heavy duty plastic sheet (perhaps even laid over loose sheets of hardboard) as a base for your load.

Access

If you're concerned about your access ask the supplier to visit you and check it out before he delivers. Otherwise you could be in the embarrassing and very difficult situation of having a huge truckload of material at your front door which cannot be offloaded conveniently. If the supplier has O.K'd your access, it's his problem. Otherwise, it's yours.

Get the delivery as close to its final destination as possible. If desirable, tip your load in several heaps. It's quite amazing just how skilful most truck drivers are. They can get their trucks into quite difficult places, and judge the amount tipped off quite accurately. For instance, recently I had a 20 cubic metre load of hardwood chips delivered, and the driver quite nonchalantly dropped it in six separate locations, with different quantities in each spot. That really saved me some work. Usually, all that's required for this sort of co-operation to be obtained is normal politeness.

Some people are worried by the large quantity of mulch to be spread. Don't be. It's very light to shovel, carry or wheel, and it's easy to spread. Providing your stockpile is within reasonable distance of the 'work face' (i.e., up to 20 metres or so) an average person working fairly hard can easily put down 1 cubic metre (i.e., 10-12 square metres) in an hour. And because the work is light, children can help, and so might your friends (particularly if you offer a barbecue afterwards!).

Inspect before you buy

Especially if you buy in bulk, go and look at what you intend to order, unless you're certain there are no communications problems with your supplier.

This may be important with sand/soil, it is important with mulch,
and it's essential with bush stone, hardwood sleepers and so on. In the case of bush stone, if you're ordering a load, get some acceptable samples from the supplier (you may have to pay — but do it anyway) and use them to judge the quality of the load.

Don't pay until you've got the goods

The great majority of suppliers will accept a C.O.D. arrangement. If they won't — be careful — they should be treated with caution. However, they are entitled to ask you to accept the goods *before* they are tipped from the truck. This should provide you with ample opportunity to check that what you're getting is what you want and what you ordered.

Be there when delivery is effected

This is pretty obvious. You must be there if you're going to check the goods — but you could be optimistic and assume they'll be O.K. and leave a cheque in the letter box. (Don't!)

Another important reason for being there is to make sure that the load is placed exactly where you want it — especially if you want it dropped in more than one location.

Bear in mind that if what's delivered isn't what you ordered, you are quite within your rights to refuse to both accept and pay. You won't have trouble with reputable, well-established firms — but there are always unscrupulous operators who may try to intimidate you (if they think they'll get away with it).

Plants

Most people buy plants one or two at a time, and naturally pay full retail price.

If you are well prepared, and have checked out your nursery in advance, you'll be ready to buy a lot of plants together — maybe even hundreds.

If you approach the principal of the nursery with your list, he'll probably offer two things:

1. a discount
2. delivery
(If he doesn't offer, ask!)

He should offer both because it's a big sale and he'll save quite a bit on overheads. Let's face it, some people take half an hour to buy one small plant, and seek 20 minutes advice about where to plant it, how to look after it etc. Here are you, bright eyed and bushy tailed, all set to take a truckload (or at least a stationwagon full) *and* you know what you want. What a relief! !

However, do *not* buy so-called 'advanced plants' which are quite often 'specials' or 'sale' items. Typical offerings are eucalypts up to 1½ metres tall in a tiny container. These plants have usually outgrown their container, are root bound, and will cause you no end of trouble.

Buy small to moderate size plants. Make sure they look healthy, with new growth evident at the tips. Stems should be straight (particularly for trees), and foliage should be free from all obvious disease.

If you've taken the advice offered earlier, you'll have seen a number of nurseries, and you'll have a good feel for the general condition of the stock anyway. If the place doesn't look well run, plants *generally* aren't healthy looking, or prices are too high — you're doing business with the wrong people.

Another advantage of bulk buying is that you may well get access to stock which is not yet on display. This will give you a wider selection, and probably better prices again.

But above all, remember that nothing is cheap if it's not what you want — and you want good, healthy, well established plants. You will get a lot of pleasure if you buy good stock — and you'll be very disappointed if you don't.

Hibbertia obtusifolia

PLANTING

You may be surprised at the number of plants you have on your list — and somewhat dismayed at how much planting is in front of you.

However, remember that all your ground has been well prepared (so there won't be any hard digging), and the mulch is in place — so all you have to do is to put the plant in the ground and water it.

How long will it take?

In properly prepared ground, a reasonably experienced person can easily plant 150-200 mm (6-8 inch) pots in 10 minutes each. Small pots i.e., 50-75 mm (2-3 inches) can be done in 5 minutes.

This means two of you can easily plant 50 large pots in half a day (2 people x 4 hours x 6 pots per hour = 48). So, the task is not all that daunting.

Laying out

Buying all or most of your plants together gives you the advantage of setting out the pots in what will be their final position. You'll do this from your plan, modifying the layout a little to suit any changes or additions in your purchasing.

So, place the pots around in their planned positions. Stand back — and have a good look. Walk around among them.

Make any small adjustments you feel desirable — at all times bearing in mind the final height and spread of each plant.

Don't be disappointed if it looks a bit bare. You're planting babies, and they'll grow quickly. And don't be seduced into overplanting —

you'll end up with a mess, with shrubs growing into one another, and eventually you may have to remove several healthy plants just to make room for the others.

Once you're satisfied with your layout, you're ready to go.

You will need

· Small garden spade
· 2 plastic buckets
· Sharp knife or scissors
· Sharp secateurs
· A hose with a 'gun' nozzle (for intermittent availability of water) *or* a large watering can.
· Container of Blood & Bone fertilizer

Planting method

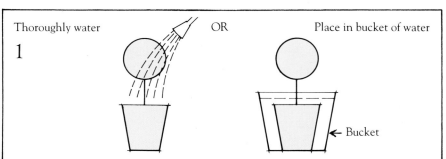

Thoroughly water

1

OR

Place in bucket of water

← Bucket

1. Thoroughly water the plant the evening before you plant so that you're certain the plant is moist, but excess water has drained away before planting. Alternatively, a good method is to place the plant, still in its container, in a bucket of water. Depth of water is to be adequate to completely cover soil in container. Plant should stay in water until air bubbles cease rising; this usually takes a minute or two.

2. *Carefully* remove mulch from area in which plant is to be located. The area to be cleared of mulch is a circle about 200-300 mm (8-12 inches) larger in diameter than that of the plant container.

Just heap the mulch up next to the cleared area. It will be replaced shortly.

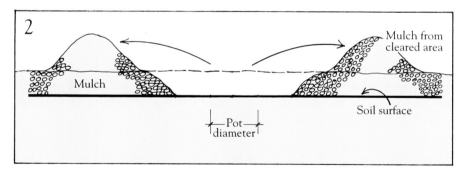

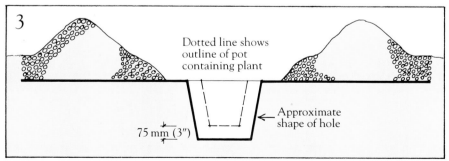

3. Carefully dig a hole about 100 mm (4 inches) larger in diameter than that of the container and about 75 mm (3 inches) deeper than the depth of soil in the pot. Place soil from hole in your empty bucket.

Hole sides should be nearly vertical.

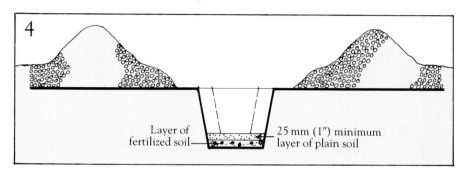

Fertilizer table

Pot size (diameter)		Fertilizer quantity
mm	inches	
50	2	1 teaspoon
100	4	2 teaspoons
150	6	1 tablespoon
200	8	2 tablespoons

4. There is some disagreement as to whether or not fertilizer should be added at the planting stage. After an examination of the evidence, I'm for it. However, it must be done carefully — the raw fertilizer must not touch the plant roots, and the quantity must be watched. Use only the fertilizer recommended. Blood & Bone is a safe but effective slow release fertilizer.

Mix the recommended amount of fertilizer (see table) with about 50 mm (2 inches) of soil in an empty plant container about the same size as the one you're planting. Place this mixture in the bottom of the hole, and level it out. Now place a further layer of ordinary (i.e., unfertilized) soil over the mixture to bring it to the correct height for the plant to be level with the surface. This further layer should be not less than 25 mm (1 inch) thick.

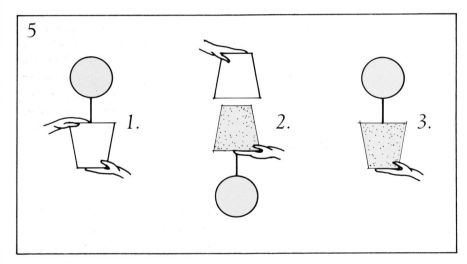

5. Remove plant from container.

If the container is a plastic pot, the pot is easily loosened by flexing it gently. If the container is plastic sheet, cutting it with a knife or scissors down two opposite sides will make it easy to remove. Place your left hand over the top of the pot, with the stem between your 2nd and 3rd fingers. Up-end the plant, and, while holding the plant and root ball with your left hand, remove the container with your right.

Hold the root ball with your right hand, and invert the plant to its correct position.

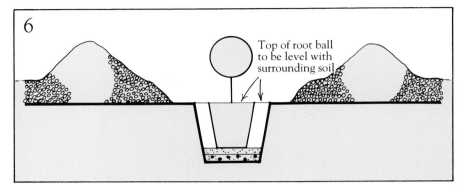

6. Carefully place plant in hole. The plant stem should be vertical, even if you are planting on a slope. The top of the root ball should be level with the surrounding soil. If it is too high, remove soil from the hole. If it is too low, place extra soil in the hole until the level is correct.

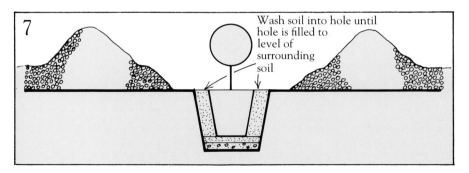

7. Loosely pack soil from bucket around root ball until the plant is properly located. Thoroughly soak this soil and 'wash' it into place with a gentle jet from the hose or watering can.

Wash sufficient soil into the hole until it is completely filled. The top of the root ball should now be level with the surrounding surface.

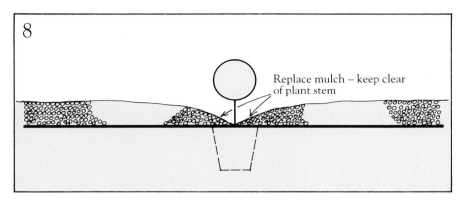

8

Replace mulch – keep clear of plant stem

8. Carefully replace the mulch. But do not pack it around the stem, as this may cause 'collar rot'.

You're finished!

Bear in mind that you will always have surplus soil when planting, so you'll need somewhere else to put it.

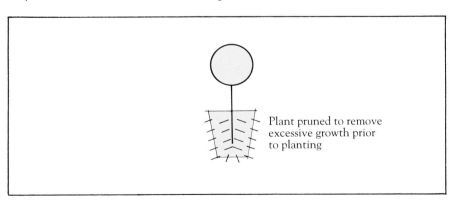

Plant pruned to remove excessive growth prior to planting

Important note

Most plants can be planted directly as indicated. They will stand reasonably rough handling, although it's desirable to keep the root ball intact.

However, plants which have spent too long in the pot will be somewhat 'root bound'. Unless something is done, they may suffer poor development, or not develop at all. Here's what to do.

It's normal on removal of the root ball from the pot to see root growth around the edges of the soil containing the roots. If this looks excessive to you — and you'll just have to learn the hard way here — tease the roots away from the edge of the soil, and prune any over long roots with your secateurs. Such pruning — done in moderation — will not harm your plant. When you've finished this operation, your plant will look something like the diagram. Don't forget that this treatment is usually unnecessary.

Staking

As a general rule, it is undesirable and unnecessary to stake newly planted plants. However, this is not so always. Sometimes it *is* desirable and occasionally it's essential to stake. This is discussed under 'Maintenance'.

Watering

As soon as you've finished planting, water the whole area with a sprinkler thoroughly. Leave the sprinkler on for a couple of hours.

See the chapter on 'Maintenance' for further watering advice.

MAINTENANCE

The whole thrust of this book is to provide you with a 'minimum' maintenance garden. But 'minimum' doesn't mean 'nil'!

Maintenance can, however, be divided into two categories — essential and desirable. Ignore the 'essential' elements at your peril. If you undertake the 'desirable' aspects you'll find it won't take long and you will be well rewarded.

Categories are:

Essential
Watering
Weeding

Desirable
Fertilizing
Pruning
Pest & Disease Control
Mulching
Staking
· Note: Sometimes, staking is 'essential'.

Let's look at each of these aspects in turn.

Watering

Regular watering is essential only with young plants, or if you've planted plants which need a good water supply and you are in an arid area. Once plants are well established, they'll be able to withstand long periods without water providing, of course, you have mulched your garden properly.

One of the main purposes of mulch is to keep soil moist by preventing excessive evaporation. You'll be surprised by just how moist well mulched soil is even after long periods without watering.

The basic rules are:

1. Water only when necessary.
Check the moisture of the soil by moving the mulch aside, and feeling the soil with your finger. If it's moist — you *probably* don't need to water. However — particularly in hot weather — you should check in a few locations.

2. When you do water, water thoroughly.
The objective here is to thoroughly soak the soil to encourage deep rooting. Many light waterings (with a hand held hose, for instance) will encourage root growth near the surface, as water will not penetrate deeply, and the roots will go after the moisture.

So, it's best to use a sprinkler, sprinkler system, or soaker hose. You can easily cut down on the time involved by installing one of the many excellent inground sprinkler systems available commercially. They are cheap, easily installed, and effective.

Alternatively, use a permanent soaker hose installation. While this doesn't look as nice as an 'inground' system, it's more easily moved to suit changing requirements.

If you add to your 'system' one of the 'tap timer' devices you can buy at all hardware stores, you can 'set and forget'. A twist of the wrist will set your system running for an hour or two and automatically turn the water off at the end of the time you've selected.

How easy it is!

3. Water when it's cool.

Don't water during the heat of the day in summer. It's a lot better to water early in the morning or, preferably, late in the afternoon. In winter, particularly in colder areas, morning watering is best.

Finally, remember that ferns are different — they will take as much water as they can get. It's fine to water them as frequently as you wish. In fact, if they're not getting enough water, they'll soon let you know by drooping and generally looking sad.

Weeding

This is classified as 'essential' because I want to save you time and trouble again (I'm all heart, really!).

If you prepare and mulch your garden as suggested, you'll have very few weeds for years. But — there will be some. The great majority of these will come from wind blown seed which germinates in the mulch itself. As they don't have a foothold in the soil, they are very easy to remove.

So, every month or two, take a stroll around the garden and remove the undesirable aliens. Even in a large area, this will only take minutes.

As I write this, I'm looking out my window at a large mulched area of my garden which hasn't been touched for at least 2 months. I can't see any weeds, but I know that I'd find a few of the little beasts if I looked. I guess it would take 10-15 minutes to go over the 100 square metres involved — not bad, eh?

If it's all so easy, why is this classified as 'essential'? Well, the exp-lanation's easy too. Weeds, being what they are, will quickly become established and then they'll proliferate. If you let them go, you'll have a comparatively big job on your hands, and in the meantime your garden will look a mess.

So the message is — remove weeds on a regular basis. That way it won't take long and your garden will always look good.

Fertilizing

The difference between an ordinary garden and a 'good' one is fertilizer. Plants may — and often do — grow quite well without any fertilizer at all. When it's all said and done, nobody roams around the bush fertilizing natives.

On the other hand, a lot of the native plants you see in the bush are pretty miserable specimens, and you don't want that in your garden.

Strong and healthy plants look good, and are able to resist disease much better than their weaker cousins. For these reasons alone, it's worthwhile ensuring optimum conditions through the addition of fertilizer.

There are lots of excellent and suitable fertilizers available. But to eliminate confusion, I recommend only one — Blood & Bone. This is a natural slow release fertilizer which is easy to apply and gets good results.

When?

In all states except W.A., apply fertilizer in August/September — August in warmer areas, September in colder areas. In other words, apply just before spring growth.

In W.A., most plants grow during the wet winter, so apply fertilizer either in late summer or early autumn (i.e., February/March).

In the Eastern States, a second light application late in February is beneficial.

How much and method of application

We both know you're not going to carefully weigh out the fertilizer, carefully measure out 1 metre squares, and evenly distribute the fertilizer over each square.

Just the same, the right amount *is* about a small handful per square metre. So put your hand in the bag, take a small handful of fertilizer, and, as you walk around the garden, 'broadcast' the fertilizer at about this rate.

Bear in mind that small plants require a little less — big plants and trees correspondingly more.

A good rule is to start off sparingly — and see how things go. If all is well after the first major application, you can try a little more the next time around. A 'light' application is about half that already described.

Before you fertilize, water the garden well — say for a third of your normal watering time. Apply the fertilizer to the wet mulch, and then water for the rest of the cycle. For example, if you normally water for 1½ hours, water for ½ an hour before you fertilize and then for a further hour afterwards.

In spite of your best endeavours, one or more of your plants may not do too well. If this is the case, take a cutting to 'your' nursery (for by now you'll have adopted one or more) and seek advice for the specific problem.

Pruning

An essential tool in the garden is a good pair of secateurs — kept sharp. If you don't own a pair, buy one, and spend the extra couple of dollars necessary to get a set which are easy to use and do the job well.

Why prune at all? Reasons are:
1. To remove broken, dead or diseased limbs
2. To shape the plant
3. To encourage general healthy growth and, of course, 'bushiness'.

Natives respond well to pruning — for example, Grevilleas positively thrive on it. So it's highly unlikely you'll do any damage. Here are the details.

Broken, dead or diseased limbs

The cut should be vertical. This minimises water entry and rotting, and the consequent easy entry of diseases and pests. If you're going to remove the whole branch, cut as close to the trunk as you can. This looks better, and gives the plant a chance to cover the wound with bark.

Removal of larger branches will require a saw, of course. 'Undercut' the branch first, to ensure that when it is cut through it doesn't peel the bark from the tree. A rope can also be helpful in holding the branch in position until it is cut through. Removal of large, heavy branches can be dangerous to life and property — so be careful. Always have assistance, control the branch with a rope and — if it's really beyond you — call in an expert.

Shaping the plant

As I've said before, it's your garden. If a plant is growing in a shape or to a size that doesn't suit, it's your prerogative to change it. Pruning may be the answer (but see also 'Staking'). However, it's highly desirable to start when the plant is young. Cutting to shape early will eliminate the 'woody' look that results when mature plants are cut back heavily.

Encouraging healthy growth and 'bushiness'

Pruning is best done generally when flowering is finished. After all, you don't want to cut off developing flowers, do you? But 'tip pruning' can be done nearly all year. This is simple, and involves either pulling out (with your fingers) or cutting off (with secateurs) the growth tips. This promotes 'lateral growth' i.e., where there was one stem, you'll now get two or more. This makes the plant more bushy and dense. Of course, you can be shaping the plant at the same time.

Note that 'tip' pruning also stimulates new root growth.

Finally, if you're getting rid of diseased prunings, don't use them as mulch or compost. Burn them or take them to the rubbish tip.

Pest and disease control

If you knew how many pests and diseases are ready to prey on your plants, you'd put in wall to wall concrete. And yet the plants in the bush all manage to do quite well — so how come?

There is a lot of biological warfare going on in your garden all the time — A eats B, B eats C, etc — and your job is to encourage the 'goodies' who will eat the 'baddies'. For this reason, I'm against the general use of chemical sprays — they have the potential to do too much damage to the 'goodies' — often our native birds.

Most pests can be controlled manually — and easily. By this I mean squashing the offending beast (or beasts) with your fingers, or underfoot. Always use gloves, as it's a lot less messy that way and they will protect you from the things that might sting or bite — e.g., some of the caterpillars can give you a nasty sting if you brush against them with bare flesh.

A couple of pests are not so easy. 'Scale' looks like a series of white deposits on branches and leaves of a plant. You can either cut off the affected part and burn it, or scrub off the scale using an old tooth brush and soapy water.

Borers are caterpillars which burrow into a tree leaving an obvious deposit of 'sawdust' on the outside of their hole. Control of borers is difficult, but the following method can be tried. Clean the sawdust away until you can see the hole, and give the hole a quick squirt with household aerosol insect killer. Sometimes only a branch is affected, and it might be satisfactory to cut off the branch and burn it — borers and all.

Generally speaking, 'squashing' is quite effective, particularly if you're supported by the many birds you can expect to get in your garden. If you don't use sprays, you won't affect the ecology and, in particular, you won't poison your avian visitors.

At the same time, if something attacks your favourite plant and the situation appears to be getting out of control, go to your nursery. But do ask for something which is not toxic to birds and will break down quickly. Also, observe application instructions carefully to ensure your own safety.

Mulching

If you've mulched in accordance with directions, it will last for years. But any organic material will break down eventually, and you may have to remulch.

This evil day (which calls for work) can be forestalled indefinitely if you have a sufficient supply of leaves to generate your own continuing mulch augmentation programme. So put all your leaves, plant clippings etc back on the garden. However, *don't* use lawn clippings unless they are thoroughly composted.

Remove large sticks, as they'll look untidy. Small sticks can be broken up and thrown back on the garden (if you wish).

Staking

A lot of nonsense is talked and written about the use of stakes. Some 'authorities' say plants should never be staked, as it's essential for the plants to grow naturally and form a root system strong enough to cope with their environment.

All of that's fine, but what do you do when you put in a plant and it falls over? Or, you're in a windy area, and the winds keep on flattening your precious new plantings? You stake, of course. Sometimes, too, a plant won't grow in the direction you wish, and it needs to be trained. Staking is useful for this.

There is nothing wrong with staking *providing* you don't fully restrain the plant and you don't allow the stake to damage it (by being too close and rubbing against it).

Small to medium plants are very readily positioned by 30 mm (1.25 inches) square hardwood stakes. Sharpen one end of the stake, and drive it firmly in the ground with a heavy hammer (a mason's hammer is ideal). Avoid the plant roots, and keep the stake at least 150 mm (6 inches) from the plant.

Don't use wire or fine string to tie the plant to the stake. Use coarse string (venetian blind cord is good and permanent) or cloth — these materials won't cut into the plant. Old panty hose and stockings are good — but you need a supply source if, like me, you don't wear them yourself.

Use a 'figure eight' (see diagram) knot to tie the plant to the stake:

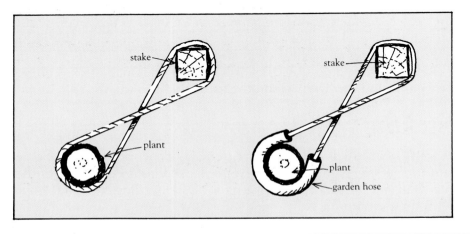

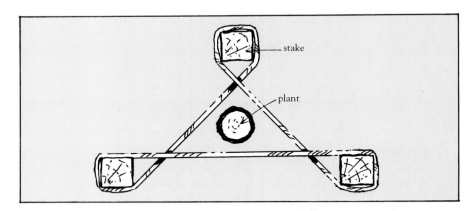

If possible, locate the tie vertically by placing it just above a branch on the plant. If this is inconvenient, fix the tie to the stake with a nail or staple. Sometimes, it will be necessary to use two or even three stakes to achieve your objective. This is fine — but ensure always that stakes are not too close to the trunk and the plant can move.

Note: In this system, the tie is not attached to the plant stem at all.

You may be concerned that your tie will cut into the plant. If this is so, pass the tie through a section of garden hose about 150 mm (6 inches) long as protection. (See diagram.)

Don't overlook the fact that you may be able to position, train or straighten your plant by tying it to a nearby tree or shrub or even a fence or wall. If you use this method, where the support could be a metre or more from the plant, it will not be feasible to use the 'figure eight' tie.

Simply put a loop in the end of the tie around the plant — but make sure it's not tight — the loop should be at least twice the diameter of the plant trunk, and should be knotted so that it can't slip.

Check your stakes occasionally. Remove them as soon as you can. Reposition ties when desirable, and change the position of the stake if you think it necessary.

GREVILLEAS

Proteus was the prophetic old man of the sea in Greek Mythology and shepherd of the sea's flocks. One of his attributes was that he was able to change his shape at will — a lion, a serpent, a leopard, a boar, a tree, fire, water etc.

So what has this to do with Grevilleas, you ask? Well, apart from the fact that I thought you'd be interested in Proteus' activities, Grevilleas belong to the Protea family — named after Proteus.

The origin of this family name is very apt for Grevilleas as they come in an enormously wide variety. While there are about 250-270 known species, many come in several forms, so that the effective number of Grevilleas is upwards of 1,000.

Grevillea rosmarinifolia

Already, Grevilleas are one of the most popular plants in Australia. I think it would be impossible to find a native garden without several specimens. They range from the towering and beautiful silky oak (G. Robusta) through many beautiful shrubs to luxuriant ground covers. They vary widely in their flower colours, flower type, climatic tolerance, growth habits and foliage.

Many are easy to grow (providing the location is suitable), they propagate from seed and cuttings, and require little attention. Birds are very attracted to them by their copious nectar production. Some species flower all year round, and others can be found which flower in spring, summer, autumn and winter.

All in all, Grevilleas are really something!

Of special interest to new gardeners is that many Grevilleas are very fast growing. They tolerate and, in fact, thrive on pruning, so you can shape them to your heart's content. Most varieties are resistant to wind, so they can be used as screen plants for more fragile species, and disease is rarely a problem.

There is a large range of colour — virtually *every* colour including red, pink, green, orange, yellow, white, black, grey etc. Even multicoloured forms are available.

The 3 main flower types are:
Spider flowers
Toothbrush flowers
Brush flowers
Additionally, there are many different leaf types. Some foliage is prickly, some is soft. Foliage colours vary widely, adding further interest.

Hybrids

A hybrid occurs when two species are crossed. This occurs naturally, but in recent times, many new Grevillea hybrids have been created deliberately.

Some hybrids are among the most exciting of the Grevilleas. Examples are 'Robyn Gordon', 'Sandra Gordon', 'Misty Pink', and 'Boongala Spinebill' — but there are many more.

Typically, hybrids are more vigorous and hardy than their parents. They grow faster, tolerate climatic extremes better and are more disease resistant. Some hybrids (e.g., 'Robyn Gordon' and 'Ned Kelly') flower all year round.

Many of the Grevilleas you will be offered will be hybrids — generally speaking, you can be confident of good results. But don't rush to buy each new introduction promoted by nurseries or magazines. Some are not worth having, or will be unsatisfactory in your area. Give them time to prove themselves, unless you are prepared to risk disappointment. The best will be available always; poor varieties will disappear from the market.

Grevillea 'Robyn Gordon'

Grevillea 'Red Dragon'

General

Grevilleas like full sun, but some will grow in part shade. They will not grow in full shade.

A light, well-aerated soil is best, although some types tolerate clayey soils. Good drainage is essential. Elevated beds are an excellent way of achieving this.

Selection

Because of the wide variety available and the many different conditions applicable in our country, it's best to check what grows well in your area (by personal inspection) and ask advice from your nursery. There are quite a few listed in this book, and of all natives, Grevilleas are worth a try providing conditions are at least reasonable.

BIRDS

One of the great attractions of a native garden is that the fruit and flowers it produces and the insects it harbours will attract native birds.

There are over 500 species of birds which breed and live within Australia. Of these, the main families are honeyeaters, parrots and finches.

Many Australian birds have glorious plumage; others beautiful songs. All are attractive in their own unique way. Certainly, they are an asset to any garden.

The requirements of birds are simple: food, water and shelter. If all of these are available in your garden, you will soon have your own bird population, although most will be visitors.

Pets

Birds can do without cats and dogs — but you might not want to part with your pet. Dogs are not really dangerous, although it helps to train them not to bark and carry on at the sight of a visiting bird.

Cats are different. Birds are a natural prey, and only a fat and lazy (or maybe old) cat will pass up a fresh meal of bird — although most of the time they seem to kill for fun. The corrective action you can take is threefold:

1. Tie a bell to the cat's collar (bells are available at pet shops). The tinkle of the bell will warn the bird of the cat's presence, and enable the bird to take prompt evasive action.

2. If you wish to feed the birds, ensure that the cat cannot get to the food tray and hence the birds. (See later for a suitable design.)

3. If you want to make a tree 'cat-proof', wrap around the trunk a piece of light sheet metal (galvanized iron or aluminium) about 900 mm (3 feet) high, and nail or tie it securely to the tree. Ensure that it is high enough so that the cat can't jump over it. When selecting your tree, don't overlook possible access by the cat from an adjacent roof or fence or another tree.

Water

While it's probable birds in your area will be able to get a drink elsewhere, a reliable supply of fresh, clean water in your garden is a definite attraction.

Ayleen Black's garden at Belmont, N.S.W.

So that cats can't reach the birds, it's best to use a pedestal type bird bath as in diagram A.

Preferably, the bath should be place under a 'cat-proof' tree, so that the birds can easily reach safety if they are alarmed.

Birds will use the bath year-round to drink and bathe. You'll have a lot of fun watching their antics as they look at themselves in the water and take their shower.

To help birds find the bath initially, hang a hose from a tree so that water drips into the bath. The noise of the drip will alert the birds to the presence of water. If you're going away for a while, or you otherwise don't have time to replace the water, the dripping hose approach will ensure a continuous supply of clear water. Just the same, it's a good idea to clean out the bath occasionally.

Food

Food is, of course, an absolute necessity. Ideally, birds should obtain their food from natural sources. This way, they'll have a balanced diet and won't lose their ability to forage for themselves.

So, your garden should include plants which will attract birds because of their food value. Such plants are noted in the Chapter 'The Plants'.

Just the same, you may wish to do *some* feeding — if only to attract the birds your way initially. If this is the case, you should provide a food tray mounted on a post. (See diagram B.)

A good material for this construction is cedar, which is light, easy to work and highly resistant to decay. The ledge around the tray is to prevent food falling off and making a mess on the ground. If you have a cat, 'cat-proof' the post with a piece of light sheet metal as described earlier.

The type of food you supply is basically determined by the requirement of the two main classes of birds: nectar feeders and others. Nec-

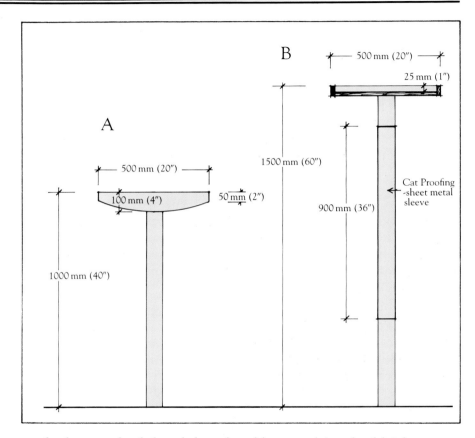

tar feeders can be fed with bread and honey or (preferably) honey in water. A special mixture — 'German Paste' — can be made from mixing together equal parts of malted dripping, honey, ground lentils and instant oats. This is a good all round food suitable for most birds.

Seed eaters will be delighted with millet and sunflower seed. Cheese and diced apple will also be popular.

If you are really interested in the welfare of the birds, though, you will plant with a view to eventually providing a good natural source of food — and shelter, the next topic.

Shelter

Essentially, birds need shelter to protect them from birds of prey and for nesting.

All birds are camouflaged to blend with their natural habitat, and make sighting difficult for predators. Generally, we see birds when they move — if they remain still, they're very hard to distinguish. If a predator is about, the natural tendency for the small birds is to 'freeze' in the expectation that they won't be seen.

Provision of trees and various shrubs will provide this shelter. Shelter for nesting is another matter.

Next to survival, a bird's greatest urge is to reproduce. Naturally, birds seek a well-protected site for their nest so that their eggs and young are well protected.

Smaller birds will nest in quite small shrubs and trees — providing they are dense and — often preferred — prickly. Naturally, the obvious presence of a full time predator (e.g., the family cat) will deter any prudent bird from settling in.

Some of the larger birds may be persuaded to nest by the provision of hollow logs fastened well up in trees. Depending on whether these are placed vertically or horizontally will be the species likely to nest.

If you wish to try this, use logs about 150-200 mm (6-8 inches) in diameter, with a hole diameter of 30-50 mm (1.25-2 inches). Cut one end square, and close it with a piece of sawn timber. Then strap it to the tree with wire or metal trapping. Place some loam in the bottom of the log to give it a natural appearance. (See diagram C.)

Place the log well up from the ground — within reason, the higher the better. 5-6 metres (16-20 feet) should be satisfactory.

Alternatively, you can make up a nest box. Important aspects are waterproofness, ventilation (at the top) and drainage (at the bottom). A typical box is shown below (Diagram D).

None of these things takes long, they're fun, and — most important — your efforts may be rewarded with a family. Some birds will nest in the same place year after year — you might win permanent residents.

Be careful that unwanted birds don't take over. You don't want starlings, for instance, or sparrows. Chase them off vigorously.

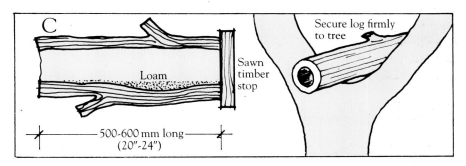

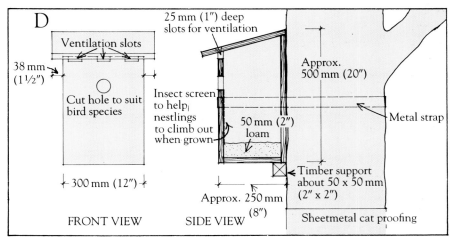

IF NOW YOU'RE HOOKED

Once you've reached the stage where your garden is established, undoubtedly you'll feel very pleased with yourself — and why not? It's quite an achievement to build your own garden, and if you've followed all the steps, it will look great (if a little bare at first), and all you *have* to do is watch it grow and potter about in it.

Of course, some of your spare time can be spent in watching the neighbours mow their lawns, get rid of their grass clippings, dig out weeds, apply fertilizer and so on.

But it's quite likely you'll be seized with the urge to do more. This may be more than you can bear. If this is the case — you're hooked!

Luckily, there are many ways in which you can satisfy your compulsion. You can even stop right now without suffering serious withdrawal symptoms. Or, you can do a little more, a lot more or allow native gardening to become a consuming passion. Whichever course you choose is completely acceptable.

On the assumption that you will want to go further, here's what to do.

First, join the Society for Growing Australian Plants (SGAP). Membership is inexpensive, and a special rate is available for those on fixed incomes and students.

The SGAP undertakes a number of activities including:

· Publication of a regular newsletter (posted free to members)
· Arranging exhibitions and displays of native plants
· A free 'Seed Service' to members
· Provision of propagating aids (tubes, pots, peat moss, hormone cutting powder etc.)
· Arranging outings for members
· Garden competitions
· A book service (books may be purchased at a number of events, or by mail order)

Additionally, there are a number of local groups who have regular informal meetings (usually monthly), often with a guest speaker, and who arrange various activities of interest to native plant lovers.

From time to time, functions are held at which plants are bought and sold (at very low prices) and, of course, arrangements can be made with other members to 'swap'.

Your participation in the SGAP can be at any level — it's up to you. You may be content simply to read the newsletter. On the other hand, you may find you are interested in being much more involved. After all, they're nice people — they're interested in native plants, just like you!

You'll find their phone number in your Telecom Directory — but if you're not in a capital city or large regional centre, you may have to make enquiries at the State (Regional) Office or your favourite native plant nursery. Note that in W.A. enquiries should be directed to the West Australian Wildflower Soc. (Inc.).

One of the fascinating aspects of native gardening is propagation i.e., growing your own plants from seed or cuttings. Many natives are easy to grow — but many are very devious, a result of their need to cope with this sometimes harsh land of ours. Some of the mysteries remain unsolved today, baffling even the real experts. Growing some of the difficult species is a real challenge.

You can propagate as simply as placing a few seeds in the ground. Or, you can build a basic propagation frame in your garden at very low cost in terms of time and money. From this you can move to a bush or shade house or even to a glass house.

There are many excellent books on native plants. Some of these are listed in 'Books worth reading'. However, when you are buying books, be careful not to buy those with lots of pretty pictures of plants which — while perhaps very attractive — are either unavailable or impossible to grow except in highly specialised environments.

All the books recommended are worthwhile and may be purchased with confidence. Naturally, there are others in this category — the list is selective rather than exhaustive.

The National Botanic Gardens in Canberra publish an excellent series of booklets entitled *Growing Native Plants*. These are well produced, with excellent colour photographs, and of course, are authoritative. The series can be purchased from the Gardens, the SGAP and many book shops.

In conclusion, there is much to do if you wish. But the degree of involvement is entirely up to you — if you wish to spend your time reading a book in your near maintenance free garden — that's fine. On the other hand, if you want to learn more and become deeply involved in an extremely fascinating subject, and make many interesting new friends in the process, the way is easy.

Melaleuca radula

THE PLANTS

Characteristics at a glance

On the following pages is a table listing 464 plants selected for your consideration. They are in alphabetical order by botanical name, and are numbered consecutively. The illustrated section, 'Descriptions' uses the same numbering system.

Select plants from the table which seem appropriate for your purpose, and then check with the illustrated section for further information. You will then be able to evaluate your choice reasonably effectively.

However, nothing is better than viewing a specimen 'in the flesh' (or should I say 'in the foliage'?). It's a big help if you can view a mature specimen of a plant in which you're interested.

Be aware that no two plants of the same species are identical. Like people, plants are individuals. And also like people, their development will depend to a large extent on their environment, and the care they are given. So, don't expect your plant to look exactly the same as the one you saw up the street. Yours *will* be different — it may be 'better' or 'worse', but it won't be the same.

Finally, a few comments about size. The heights given for some of the trees may surprise you, in that they might be smaller than you'd expect. It is a fact that, generally speaking, trees grown in cultivation don't reach the maximum height the species achieves in the bush.

The figures given are those which can be expected in your garden in good conditions.

Don't be unduly frightened by what sounds like a high tree. Often, people get the wrong impression of height, and think trees will be a lot bigger than is the case. Bulk is important too. Eucalyptus citriodora (Lemon Scented Gum) is a good example of a tall tree which, because it drops its lower branches as it grows, takes up very little room in the garden. Its canopy is very delicate and graceful, and, in spite of its vertical height, it is quite appropriate to plant three or four together within 1½-2 metres of one another.

Generally, the maximum expected height of a species is given. If a shrub may grow to a 'small' or 'medium' height, it is classified as 'medium'. On the other hand, a plant which could end up as either a 'large shrub' or 'small tree' may be listed as both.

'Clump' plants which do not take a shrubby habit have been omitted from the height columns altogether.

Important Note: In the individual description of a plant, features covered in the table may not be mentioned. This is an important reason for using the table *with* the descriptions when making your selection.

Study the 'Key to symbols' well. The symbols are simple, easy to understand, and easy to remember. But it's important that they convey to you exactly what's intended.

Key to symbols

 Showy in flower

Striking (feature) plant because of flowers or foliage

Suitable for cut flowers

Bird attracting

Suitable for tubs

Suitable for hedge or windbreak

Grows well in wet ground

Will resist reasonable frosts of at least -5°C

Grows in full sun

Grows in partly shaded conditions

Grows in full shade

Suitable for coastal (salt spray) conditions

Ground cover

Climber

Shrubs

Small — less than 1 metre (3 ft.) high

Medium — between 1 metre (3 ft.) & 3 metres (10 ft.)

Large — over 3 metres (10 ft.)

Trees

Small — up to 10 metres (33 ft.)

Large — more than 10 metres (33 ft.)

Characteristics at a glance

	Showy	Striking	Cut flowers	Bird	Tubs	Hedge	Wet ground	Frost	Full sun	Part shade	Full shade	Coastal	Ground cover	Climber	Small shrub	Med shrub	Large shrub	Small tree	Large tree
1. **Abarema** *grandiflora*		●		✓	✓					◐	●								✓
2. Abarema *sapindoides*	✓	●		✓	✓					◐	●							✓	
3. **Acacia** *acinacea*	✓	●		✓	✓			▲	☀							✓			
4. Acacia *aculeatissima*	✓	●		✓	✓				☀				═		✓				
5. Acacia *adunca*	✓	●		✓				▲	☀								✓		
6. Acacia *ambligona*	✓	●		✓	✓				☀				═						
7. Acacia *baileyana*	✓	●		✓		✓		▲	☀									✓	
8. Acacia *boormani*	✓	●		✓	✓			▲	☀							✓			

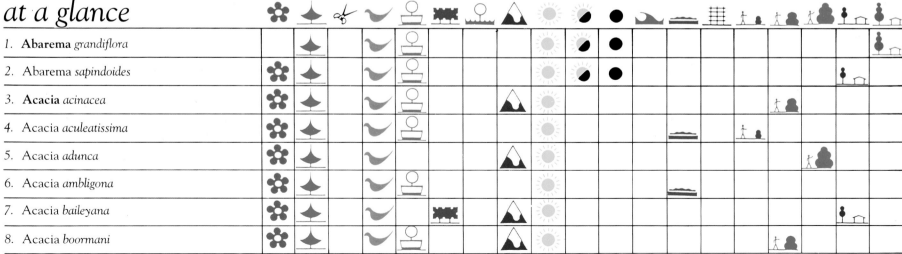

43

#	Species	🌼 flowers	🔸 spike	✂ prune	⌒ phyllode	🪴 tub	🌳 hedge	💧 water	⛰ hardy	☀ full sun	🌤 part sun	● shade	〰 coastal	▭ ground	▦ trellis	🧍 1m	🧍+shrub	🧍+shrub	🧍+lg shrub	🌲+house sm	🌲+house tall
9.	Acacia *buxifolia*	●	●		●	●	●		●	●							●				
10.	Acacia *calamifolia*	●	●		●				●	●							●				
11.	Acacia *cardiophylla*	●	●		●		●		●	●							●				
12.	Acacia *cultriformis*	●	●		●	●	●		●	●							●				
13.	Acacia *dealbarta*	●	●		●		●		●	●										●	
14.	Acacia *decora*	●	●		●					●							●				
15.	Acacia *decurrens*	●	●	✂	●		●		●	●	●									●	
16.	Acacia *drummondi*	●	●	✂	●					●						●					
17.	Acacia *elata*		●		●		●		●	●	●										●
18.	Acacia *elongata*	●	●		●	●		●	●	●	●						●				
19.	Acacia *fimbriata*	●	●		●	●	●		●	●	●								●		
20.	Acacia *glaucescens*		●		●		●		●	●											●
21.	Acacia *glaucoptera*		●		●	●			●	●						●					
22.	Acacia *gracilifolia*	●	●		●	●			●	●							●				
23.	Acacia *howitti*				●	●	●		●	●									●		
24.	Acacia *iteaphylla*	●	●		●	●	●		●	●							●				
25.	Acacia *kettlewelliae*	●	●		●					●									●	●	
26.	Acacia *lanigera*	●	●		●					●						●					
27.	Acacia *linifolia*	●	●		●				●	●	●						●				

#	Species	flowers	tree form	scissors	wavy leaf	potted	hedge	ground cover	triangle	sun	seed	black circle	dune	flat bar	grid	person+small	person+medium	person+large	tree+house sm	tree+house lg
28.	Acacia *longifolia*	✓	✓		✓	✓	✓	✓	✓	✓	✓		✓				✓			
29.	Acacia *longifolia var. sophorae*				✓	✓	✓	✓	✓				✓				✓			
30.	Acacia *mearnsi*	✓	✓		✓		✓		✓	✓									✓	
31.	Acacia *melanoxylon*	✓	✓		✓		✓		✓	✓	✓									✓
32.	Acacia *myrtifolia*				✓				✓	✓	✓					✓				
33.	Acacia *oxycedrus*	✓	✓		✓		✓		✓	✓							✓			
34.	Acacia *parramattensis*	✓	✓		✓		✓		✓	✓									✓	
35.	Acacia *pendula*	✓	✓		✓		✓			✓									✓	
36.	Acacia *podalyriifolia*	✓	✓		✓	✓	✓		✓	✓	✓							✓	✓	
37.	Acacia *pravissima*	✓	✓		✓	✓			✓	✓				✓				✓		
38.	Acacia *prominens*	✓	✓		✓				✓		✓								✓	
39.	Acacia *pycnantha*	✓	✓		✓		✓		✓	✓							✓		✓	
40.	Acacia *saligna*	✓	✓		✓		✓		✓	✓			✓						✓	
41.	Acacia *spectabilis*	✓	✓		✓	✓			✓	✓								✓		
42.	Acacia *suaveolens*				✓	✓			✓		✓		✓				✓			
43.	Acacia *terminalis*	✓	✓		✓	✓	✓		✓	✓							✓			
44.	Acacia *uncinata*	✓	✓		✓	✓					✓						✓			
45.	Acacia *vestita*	✓	✓		✓	✓	✓		✓	✓							✓			
46.	**Acmena** *Smithi*	✓	✓		✓	✓	✓	✓		✓	✓	✓					✓		✓	

#	Species
47.	**Actinotus** *helianthi*
48.	**Adenanthos** *barbigerus*
49.	Adenanthos *obovatus*
50.	**Agonis** *flexuosa*
51.	Agonis *juniperina*
52.	**Allocasuarina** *torulosa*
53.	**Angophora** *bakeri*
54.	Angophora *costata*
55.	Angophora *hispida*
56.	**Anigozanthus** *flavidus*
57.	Anigozanthus *humilis*
58.	Anigozanthus *manglesi*
59.	Anigozanthus *viridis*
60.	**Araucaria** *bidwilli*
61.	Araucaria *cunninghami*
62.	**Archontophoenix** *cunninghamiana*
63.	**Astartia** *fascicularis*
64.	Astartia *heteranthera*
65.	**Astraloma** *ciliatum*

Symbol key columns (left to right): **Flower** · **Umbrella-flower** · **Scissors** · **Leaf** · **Pot** · **Hedge** · **Lollipop** · **Triangle** · **Sun** · **Teardrop** · **Black circle** · **Wave** · **Flat layers** · **Grid** · **Person+small** · **Person+shrub** · **Person+tree** · **Tree+house** · **Tree+house (double)**

#	Species	Flower	Umbrella	Scissors	Leaf	Pot	Hedge	Lollipop	Triangle	Sun	Teardrop	Black circle	Wave	Flat layers	Grid	Person+small	Person+shrub	Person+tree	Tree+house	Tree+house 2
66.	**Austromyrtus** *dulcis*	●			●			●	●	●	●	●		●		●				
67.	Austromyrtus *tenuifolia*				●		●	●	●	●	●	●					●			
68.	**Backhousia** *citriodora*		●			●				●	●								●	
69.	Backhousia *myrtifolia*							●	●	●	●								●	
70.	**Baeckea** *densifolia*	●		●	●	●			●	●	●	●				●				
71.	Baeckea *linifolia*	●	●		●	●		●	●	●	●	●					●			
72.	Baeckea *virgata*	●		●	●	●	●	●	●	●	●							●		
73.	**Banksia** *baueri*	●	●	●	●	●				●							●			
74.	Banksia *caleyi*	●	●	●	●	●				●							●			
75.	Banksia *coccinea*	●	●	●	●	●			●	●								●		
76.	Banksia *ericifolia*	●	●	●	●	●	●	●	●	●	●		●					●		
77.	Banksia *grandis*	●	●	●	●	●			●	●								●	●	
78.	Banksia *hookerana*	●	●	●	●	●				●							●			
79.	Banksia *integrifolia*	●	●	●	●	●	●		●	●	●		●						●	
80.	Banksia *marginata*	●	●	●	●	●	●		●	●	●		●						●	
81.	Banksia *media*	●	●	●	●	●			●	●			●				●			
82.	Banksia *petiolaris*	●	●	●	●	●				●						●				
83.	Banksia *prostrata*	●	●	●	●	●				●				●		●				
84.	Banksia *repens*	●	●	●	●	●				●				●		●				

#	Species
85.	Banksia *robur*
86.	Banksia *serrata*
87.	Banksia *serratifolia (aemula)*
88.	Banksia *spinulosa* (syn. B. collina)
89.	**Bauera** *rubioides*
90.	Bauera *sessiliflora*
91.	**Beaufortia** *macrostemon*
92.	Beaufortia *sparsa*
93.	**Billardiera** *scandens*
94.	**Blandfordia** *grandiflora*
95.	Blandfordia *punicea*
96.	**Boronia** *anemonifolia*
97.	Boronia *denticulata*
98.	Boronia *floribunda*
99.	Boronia *heterophylla*
100.	Boronia *ledifolia*
101.	Boronia *megastigma*
102.	Boronia *molloyae*
103.	Boronia *muelleri*

No.	Plant	❀	◆	✂	〰	�containerized	▦hedge	🌱	▲	☀	☼	💧	●	〜	≈	▦	🧍	🧍🌳	🧍	🧍🌳	🌳	🌳🏠	🎄	🎄🏠
104.	Boronia *pinnata*	❀	◆	✂	〰	⌓		🌱	▲	☀		💧	●					🧍🌳						
105.	Boronia *serrulata*	❀	◆	✂		⌓			▲	☀		💧	●					🧍						
106.	Boronia *spathulata*								▲	☀		💧	●					🧍						
107.	**Brachychiton** *acerifolius*	❀	◆			⌓				☀		💧	●										🎄	🏠
108.	Brachychiton *discolor*	❀								☀													🎄	🏠
109.	Brachychiton *rupestre*		◆			⌓			▲	☀		💧	●										🎄	🏠
110.	**Brachycome** *multifida*					⌓		🌱	▲	☀					≈			🧍						
111.	Brachycome *sp.* (scapiformis)					⌓		🌱	▲	☀					≈									
112.	Brachycome *sp.* 'Pilliga' (affin. *melanocarpa*)	❀				⌓		🌱	▲	☀					≈									
113.	**Brachysema** *lanceolatum*	❀			〰	⌓	▦		▲	☀					≈				🧍🌳					
114.	Brachysema *latifolium*				〰	⌓			▲	☀					≈									
115.	**Buckinghamia** *celsissima*	❀	◆			⌓				☀		💧										🧍🏠		
116.	**Bursaria** *spinosa*							🌱		☀		💧	●						🧍🌳					
117.	**Callistemon** 'Burgundy'	❀			〰	⌓	▦		▲	☀									🧍🌳					
118.	Callistemon 'Candy Pink'	❀			〰	⌓	▦		▲	☀									🧍🌳					
119.	Callistemon *citrinus*	❀		✂	〰	⌓	▦	🌱	▲	☀											🧍🌳			
120.	Callistemon *citrinus* 'Anzac'	❀	◆	✂	〰	⌓	▦	🌱	▲	☀								🧍						
121.	Callistemon *citrinus* 'Australflora Firebrand'	❀	◆	✂	〰	⌓	▦	🌱	▲	☀									🧍🌳					
122.	Callistemon *citrinus* 'Endeavour'	❀	◆	✂	〰	⌓	▦	🌱	▲	☀											🧍🌳			

#	Species
123.	Callistemon 'Harkness'
124.	Callistemon 'Kings Park Special'
125.	Callistemon 'Lilacinus'
126.	Callistemon 'Mauve Mist'
127.	Callistemon pallidus
128.	Callistemon paludosus
129.	Callistemon pinifolius
130.	Callistemon polandi
131.	Callistemon 'Reeves Pink'
132.	Callistemon sieberi
133.	Callistemon speciosus
134.	Callistemon subulatus
135.	Callistemon 'Tinaroo'
136.	Callistemon viminalis
137.	Callistemon v. 'Captain Cook'
138.	Callistemon v. 'Dawson River'
139.	Callistemon v. 'Hannah Ray'
140.	Callistemon v. 'Hen Camp Creek'
141.	Callistemon v. 'Prolific'

142.	Callistemon v. 'Running River'
143.	Callistemon v. 'Western Glory'
144.	Callistemon *species* 'Baroondah'
145.	Callistemon *species* 'Injune'
146.	**Callitris** *endlicheri*
147.	Callitris *hugeli*
148.	Callitris *macleayana*
149.	Callitris *rhomboidea*
150.	**Calocephalus** *browni*
151.	**Calothamnus** *quadrifidus*
152.	Calothamnus *villosus*
153.	**Calytrix** *sullivani*
154.	Calytrix *tetragona*
155.	**Carpobrotus** *glaucescens*
156.	**Cassia** *aciphylla*
157.	Cassia *artemisoides*
158.	**Casuarina** *cunninghamiana*
159.	Casuarina *glauca*
160.	Casuarina *nana*

No.	Species
161.	Casuarina *stricta*
162.	**Ceratopetalum** *gummiferum*
163.	**Chamelaucium** *uncinatum*
164.	**Chorizema** *cordatum*
165.	**Clematis** *aristata*
166.	**Conostylis** *aculeata*
167.	**Correa** *alba*
168.	Correa *decumbens*
169.	Correa *pulchella*
170.	Correa *reflexa*
171.	**Crowea** *exalata*
172.	Crowea *saligna*
173.	**Cupaniopsis** *anacardioides*
174.	**Dampiera** *diversifolia*
175.	Dampiera *sericantha*
176.	**Darwinia** *citriodora*
177.	**Dianella** *tasmanica*
178.	**Dillwynia** *floribunda*
179.	**Diplarrena** *moraea*

180.	**Dodonaea** *viscosa*					●	●		▲	☀							●			
181.	**Doryanthes** *excelsa*	✿	◆		～	●		●	▲	☀	◗	●					●			
182.	**Dryandra** *polycephala*	✿	◆	✂	～	●				☀							●			
183.	**Eleocarpus** *reticulatus*		◆		～	●	●	●	▲	☀	◗	●							●	
184.	**Epacris** *impressa*	✿		✂	～	●		●	▲	☀	◗	●					●			
185.	Epacris *longiflora*	✿		✂	～	●		●	▲	☀	◗	●					●			
186.	**Eremophila** *gibifolia*				～	●			▲	☀							●			
187.	Eremophila *glabra*	✿			～	●			▲	☀	◗						●			
188.	Eremophila *maculata*	✿			～	●			▲	☀	◗						●			
189.	Eremophila *polyclada*	✿		✂	～	●			▲	☀	◗						●			
190.	**Eriostemon** *myoporoides*			✂	～	●	●		▲	☀	◗						●			
191.	Eriostemon *verrucosus*			✂	～	●			▲	☀	◗	●				●				
192.	**Eucalyptus** *acaciiformis*				～		●		▲	☀									●	
193.	Eucalyptus *alpina*				～					☀									●	
194.	Eucalyptus *botryoides*				～		●	●	▲	☀			～							●
195.	Eucalyptus *caesia*	✿	◆	✂	～				▲	☀									●	
196.	Eucalyptus *calophylla*	✿	◆	✂	～		●		▲	☀										●
197.	Eucalyptus *camaldulensis*				～		●	●	▲	☀										●
198.	Eucalyptus *cinerea*		◆		～		●		▲	☀										●

#	Species	✿	⬥tree	✂	leaf	pot	hedge	fountain	▲	☀	◑	●	wave	wave2	grid	fig1	fig2	fig3	fig+shrub	tree+house	tree+house2
199.	Eucalyptus *citriodora*		●		●					☀											●
200.	Eucalyptus *cladocalyx nana*				●		●		▲	☀										●	
201.	Eucalyptus *crenulata*		●		●	●		●	▲	☀										●	
202.	Eucalyptus *curtisi*				●	●			▲	☀										●	
203.	Eucalyptus *elata*				●		●		▲	☀											●
204.	Eucalyptus *eremophila*	●			●				▲	☀										●	
205.	Eucalyptus *erythrocorys*	●	●	●	●	●				☀										●	
206.	Eucalyptus *ficifolia*	●	●	●	●				▲	☀										●	
207.	Eucalyptus *forrestiana*	●	●	●	●	●				☀										●	
208.	Eucalyptus *globulus*			●	●	●	●	●	▲	☀											●
209.	Eucalyptus *globulus var. bicostata*			●	●	●	●	●	▲	☀											●
210.	Eucalyptus *grandis*		●		●				▲	☀	◑										●
211.	Eucalyptus *grossa*			●	●		●		▲	☀										●	
212.	Eucalyptus *gummifera*				●				▲	☀											●
213.	Eucalyptus *gunni*				●					☀											●
214.	Eucalyptus *haemastoma*		●		●				▲	☀											●
215.	Eucalyptus *lehmanni*	●	●	●	●	●	●		▲	☀			●							●	
216.	Eucalyptus *leucoxylon var. macrocarpa*	●	●	●	●	●			▲	☀			●								●
217.	Eucalyptus *macrocarpa*	●	●		●					☀									●		

#	Species	❀	🌲	✂	🍃	🪴	hedge	ground	▲	☀	◑	●	🌊	boat	grid	ppl	ppl	ppl	ppl	🌳🏠	🌳🏠
218.	Eucalyptus *maculata*		●		●				●	●											●
219.	Eucalyptus *mannifera sub. sp. maculosa*		●		●		●		●	●											●
220.	Eucalyptus *microcorys*				●		●		●	●	●										●
221.	Eucalyptus *nicholi*		●		●		●		●	●										●	
222.	Eucalyptus *obtusiflora*				●					●										●	
223.	Eucalyptus *orbifolia*		●		●					●										●	
224.	Eucalyptus *papuana*		●		●															●	
225.	Eucalyptus *pauciflora*		●		●				●	●											●
226.	Eucalyptus *platypus*				●				●	●										●	
227.	Eucalyptus *ptychocarpa*	●	●		●					●											●
228.	Eucalyptus *robusta*				●		●	●	●	●			●								●
229.	Eucalyptus *saligna*		●		●			●	●	●	●										●
230.	Eucalyptus *scoparia*		●		●		●		●	●											●
231.	Eucalyptus *sideroxylon rosea*	●	●		●		●		●	●											●
232.	Eucalyptus *spathulata*		●		●	●		●	●	●										●	
233.	Eucalyptus *steedmani*	●	●		●					●										●	
234.	Eucalyptus *tereticornus*				●			●	●	●											●
235.	Eucalyptus *tetraptera*	●		●	●	●			●	●										●	
236.	Eucalyptus *torquata*	●	●	●	●	●			●	●										●	

No.	Species
237.	Eucalyptus *viminalis*
238.	**Eugenia** *wilsoni*
239.	**Eutaxia** *cuneata*
240.	Eutaxia *obovata*
241.	**Goodenia** *hederacea*
242.	**Goodia** *lotifolia*
243.	**Grevillea** *acanthifolia*
244.	Grevillea *alpina*
245.	Grevillea *aquifolium*
246.	Grevillea *arenaria*
247.	Grevillea *asplenifolia*
248.	Grevillea 'Australflora Canterbury Gold'
249.	Grevillea 'Australflora Copper Crest'
250.	Grevillea *banksi*
251.	Grevillea *baueri*
252.	Grevillea *bipinnatifida*
253.	Grevillea *biternata*
254.	Grevillea 'Boongala Spinebill'
255.	Grevillea *buxifolia*

No.	Species	✿	shrub	✂	leaf	pot	hedge	lollipop	▲	☀	◐	●	wave	layered	grid	person+seedling	person+shrub	person+tree	large shrub	house+tree	topiary
256.	Grevillea *caleyi*	●	●		●	●			●	●	●						●				
257.	Grevillea 'Canberra Gem'				●	●	●		●	●							●				
258.	Grevillea *capitellata*	●			●	●			●	●	●					●	●				
259.	Grevillea 'Cascade'	●			●	●	●		●	●									●		
260.	Grevillea *chrysophaea*	●			●	●			●	●						●	●				
261.	Grevillea 'Clearview David'				●	●	●		●	●							●				
262.	Grevillea 'Clearview Robin'				●	●			●	●							●				
263.	Grevillea *confertifolia*	●			●	●			●	●				●							
264.	Grevillea *crithmifolia*				●	●	●		●	●						●	●				
265.	Grevillea 'Crosby Morrison'	●			●	●				●							●				
266.	Grevillea 'Dargan Hill'	●			●	●				●							●				
267.	Grevillea *dielsiana*	●			●				●	●							●				
268.	Grevillea *dimorpha*	●			●	●			●	●						●	●				
269.	Grevillea *endlicherana*	●	●		●	●			●	●							●				
270.	Grevillea 'Evan's Coronet'				●	●			●	●	●						●				
271.	Grevillea *evansiana*	●			●	●			●	●							●				
272.	Grevillea *fasciculata*	●			●	●			●	●						●	●				
273.	Grevillea *floribunda*	●			●	●			●	●	●						●				
274.	Grevillea *Coastal Glow*				●		●			●							●				

57

#	Species	Symbols
275.	Grevillea *Gaudichaudi*	
276.	Grevillea *glabella*	
277.	Grevillea *glabella* 'Lara Dwarf'	
278.	Grevillea *glabella* 'Limelight'	
279.	Grevillea *glabrata*	
280.	Grevillea 'Honeycomb' ('Coochin Hills')	
281.	Grevillea 'Honey Gem'	
282.	Grevillea 'Hookerana'	
283.	Grevillea *ilicifolia*	
284.	Grevillea 'Ivanhoe'	
285.	Grevillea 'Jenkinsi'	
286.	Grevillea 'Johnsoni'	
287.	Grevillea *juncifolia*	
288.	Grevillea *juniperina*	
289.	Grevillea *juniperina* 'Austraflora Lunar Light'	
290.	Grevillea *juniperina* 'Molongolo'	
291.	Grevillea *juniperina* 'Pink Lady'	
292.	Grevillea *lanigera*	
293.	Grevillea *laurifolia*	

No.	Species	Flower	Foliage	Prune	Nectar	Container	Hedge	Standard	Rockery	Full sun	Semi shade	Shade	Coastal	Frost/flat	Lattice	Small	Medium	Large	Tree
294.	Grevillea *lavandulacea*	✿			✓	✓			▲	☀							✓		
295.	Grevillea *linearifolia*				✓				▲	☀	◑	●					✓		
296.	Grevillea *longifolia*	✿	✓	✂	✓	✓	✓		▲	☀	◑	●						✓	
297.	Grevillea 'Misty Pink'	✿	✓		✓		✓			☀							✓		
298.	Grevillea 'Ned Kelly'	✿	✓		✓	✓	✓			☀							✓		
299.	Grevillea *obtusifolia*	✿			✓	✓			▲	☀						✓			
300.	Grevillea *oleoides*	✿			✓					☀							✓		
301.	Grevillea 'Olympic Flame'	✿			✓	✓	✓			☀						✓			
302.	Grevillea 'Pink Parfait'	✿	✓		✓		✓			☀							✓		
303.	Grevillea 'Pink Pearl'	✿			✓	✓	✓		▲	☀							✓		
304.	Grevillea 'Poorinda Constance'				✓	✓	✓		▲	☀							✓		
305.	Grevillea 'Poorinda Elegance'	✿			✓	✓	✓			☀							✓		
306.	Grevillea 'Poorinda Fire Bird'	✿	✓		✓	✓				☀							✓		
307.	Grevillea 'Poorinda Hula'	✿			✓	✓				☀							✓		
308.	Grevillea 'Poorinda Leane'				✓	✓	✓			☀							✓		
309.	Grevillea 'Poorinda Queen'				✓	✓	✓		▲	☀							✓		
310.	Grevillea 'Poorinda Rondeau'	✿	✓		✓	✓	✓			☀							✓		
311.	Grevillea 'Poorinda Royal Mantle'				✓	✓			▲	☀				▬					
312.	Grevillea 'Poorinda Signet'				✓	✓				☀							✓		

#	Species	✿	🌳	✂	🐦	🪴	🌳🌳	⛲	▲	☀	◐	●	〰	▤	▦	🧍	🧍🌳	🧍🌳	🌳	🌲	🏠	🌲
313.	Grevillea *pteridifolia*	✿			🐦					☀							✓					
314.	Grevillea *quercifolia*				🐦	🪴				☀						✓						
315.	Grevillea *repens*	✿			🐦	🪴				☀				✓								
316.	Grevillea *rivularis*				🐦	🪴	🌳🌳	⛲	▲	☀	◐			✓			✓					
317.	Grevillea *robusta*	✿	🌳		🐦	🪴	🌳🌳		▲	☀	◐										✓	✓
318.	Grevillea 'Robyn Gordon'	✿	🌳	✂	🐦	🪴	🌳🌳			☀							✓					
319.	Grevillea *Rosmarinifolia*	✿			🐦	🪴	🌳🌳		▲	☀							✓					
320.	Grevillea 'Sandra Gordon'	✿	🌳		🐦					☀									✓			
321.	Grevillea *sericea*	✿	🌳		🐦	🪴			▲	☀	◐					✓						
322.	Grevillea *shiressi*			✂	🐦	🪴	🌳🌳	⛲	▲	☀							✓					
323.	Grevillea 'Shirley Howie'	✿			🐦	🪴				☀							✓					
324.	Grevillea 'Sid Cadwell'				🐦		🌳🌳			☀							✓					
325.	Grevillea *speciosa*	✿			🐦	🪴			▲	☀	◐						✓					
326.	Grevillea *thelemanniana*	✿	🌳		🐦	🪴				☀				✓								
327.	Grevillea *triloba*	✿			🐦		🌳🌳		▲	☀							✓					
328.	Grevillea *victoriae*				🐦	🪴		⛲	▲	☀							✓					
329.	Grevillea 'White Wings'	✿			🐦					☀							✓					
330.	Grevillea *wilsoni*	✿	🌳		🐦				▲	☀						✓						
331.	**Hakea** *bakerana*	✿	🌳		🐦	🪴	🌳🌳	⛲	▲	☀	◐						✓					

#	Species
332.	Hakea *cristata*
333.	Hakea *dactyloides*
334.	Hakea *francisiana*
335.	Hakea *laurina*
336.	Hakea *petiolaris*
337.	Hakea *salicifolia*
338.	Hakea *suaveolens*
339.	**Hardenbergia** *comptoniana*
340.	Hardenbergia *violacea*
341.	**Helychrysum** *baxteri*
342.	Helychrysum *bracteatum* 'Dargan Hill Monarch'
343.	Helychrysum *bracteatum* 'Diamond Head'
344.	**Helipterum** *roseum*
345.	**Hemiandra** *pungens*
346.	**Hibbertia** *astrotricha*
347.	Hibbertia *obtusifolia*
348.	Hibbertia *pedunculata*
349.	Hibbertia *scandens*
350.	**Hibiscus** *divaricatus*

351. Hibiscus *splendens*	✿	◆			⬓				☀									👤👥			
352. **Homoranthus** *darwinioides*				∿	⬓			▲	☀							👤👥				
353. Homoranthus *flavescens*				∿	⬓			▲	☀							👤👥				
354. **Hymenosporum** *flavum*	✿	◆		∿			○	▲	☀	◗	●								🌳🏠	
355. **Hypocalymma** *angustifolium*	✿		✂		⬓			▲	☀	◗	●					👤👥				
356. Hypocalymma *cordifolium*					⬓			▲	☀	◗	●					👤👥				
357. **Indigofera** *australis*								▲	☀	◗	●						👤👥			
358. **Isopogon** *anemonifolius*			✂	∿	⬓	▦		▲	☀	◗						👤👥				
359. Isopogon *anethifolius*		◆	✂	∿	⬓			▲	☀	◗						👤👥				
360. Isopogon *dubius*	✿		✂	∿	⬓			▲	☀							👤👥				
361. **Isotoma** *axillaris*	✿			∿	⬓		○		☀							👤👥				
362. **Jacksonia** *scoparia*	✿	◆		∿				▲	☀	◗									👤🌳	🌳🏠
363. **Kennedia** *eximea*	✿			∿	⬓				☀				▬	▦						
364. Kennedia *microphylla*	✿			∿	⬓				☀				▬							
365. Kennedia *prostrata*	✿			∿	⬓				☀				▬							
366. Kennedia *rubicunda.*				∿					☀	◗		🌊	▬	▦						
367. **Kunzea** *ambigua*	✿			∿	⬓	▦		▲	☀			🌊					👤👥			
368. Kunzea *baxteri*	✿		✂	∿	⬓	▦		▲	☀								👤👥			
369. Kunzea *capitata*	✿		✂	∿	⬓		○	▲	☀							👤👥				

#	Species	❀	▲	✂	〰	⊔	▦	♣	⛰	☀	◑	●	〜	≋	▦	人	人♣	人🌳	🌳⌂
370.	Kunzea *pomifera*				●	●			●	●	●			●					
371.	Kunzea sp. 'Badja carpet'				●	●			●	●	●			●					
372.	**Lagunaria** *patersoni*	●					●			●			●						●
373.	**Lambertia** *formosa*	●			●	●			●	●	●							●	
374.	**Lechenaultia** *biloba*	●	●			●			●	●						●			
375.	Lechenaultia *formosa*	●	●			●			●	●						●			
376.	**Leptospermum** *flavescens*	●			●	●	●	●	●	●	●							●	
377.	Leptospermum *flavescens* 'Pacific Beauty'	●			●	●	●	●	●	●	●			●		●			
378.	Leptospermum *laevigatum*				●		●		●	●			●					●	●
379.	Leptospermum *petersoni*				●		●			●	●							●	
380.	Leptospermum *scoparium*	●	●	●	●	●	●	●	●	●	●	●						●	
381.	**Lomandra** *longifolia*				●	●		●	●	●	●	●				●			
382.	**Lomatia** *silaifolia*	●		●					●	●	●					●			
383.	**Lophostemon** *confertus*						●	●	●	●	●								●
384.	**Melaleuca** *armillaris*		●		●	●	●	●	●	●	●	●	●					●	●
385.	Melaleuca *bracteata*				●		●	●	●	●								●	
386.	Melaleuca *bracteata* 'Golden Gem'		●		●	●	●	●	●	●							●		
387.	Melaleuca *bracteata* 'Revolution Green'		●		●		●	●	●	●							●		
388.	Melaleuca *bracteata* 'Revolution Gold'		●		●		●	●	●	●						●			

#	Species
389.	Melaleuca *capitata*
390.	Melaleuca *cuticularis*
391.	Melaleuca *diosmifolia*
392.	Melaleuca *elliptica*
393.	Melaleuca *ericifolia*
394.	Melaleuca *fulgens*
395.	Melaleuca *huegeli*
396.	Melaleuca *hypericifolia*
397.	Melaleuca *incana*
398.	Melaleuca *laterita*
399.	Melaleuca *leucadendron*
400.	Melaleuca *linariifolia*
401.	Melaleuca *megacephala*
402.	Melaleuca *nematophylla*
403.	Melaleuca *nesophila*
404.	Melaleuca *nodosa*
405.	Melaleuca *pulchella*
406.	Melaleuca *quinquenervia*
407.	Melaleuca *radula*

#	Species	✿	🌳	✂	~	🪴	hedge	std	▲	☀	◗	●	water	ground	trellis	person-sm	person-med	person-lg	tree+house
408.	Melaleuca *spatulata*	✓			✓	✓			✓	✓						✓			
409.	Melaleuca *squarrosa*	✓			✓		✓	✓	✓	✓							✓		
410.	Melaleuca *striata*	✓			✓					✓						✓			
411.	Melaleuca *styphelioides*		✓		✓		✓	✓	✓	✓	✓							✓	✓
412.	Melaleuca *thymifolia*	✓			✓	✓		✓		✓	✓					✓			
413.	Melaleuca *wilsoni*	✓			✓	✓			✓	✓				✓		✓			
414.	**Melastoma** *denticulatum*	✓				✓					✓	✓						✓	✓
415.	**Melia** *azedarach var. Australasica*				✓		✓	✓	✓	✓									✓
416.	**Micromyrtus** *ciliata*	✓			✓	✓			✓	✓				✓					
417.	**Myoporum** *debile*				✓	✓				✓				✓					
418.	**Myoporum** *parvifolium*	✓			✓	✓			✓	✓				✓					
419.	**Olearia** *phlogopappa*	✓			✓	✓		✓	✓	✓						✓			
420.	**Oxylobium** *scandens*	✓			✓	✓				✓				✓					
421.	**Pandorea** *jasminoides*	✓	✓			✓	✓		✓	✓	✓	✓			✓				
422.	Pandorea *pandorana*	✓	✓			✓	✓		✓	✓	✓	✓	✓		✓				
423.	**Patersonia** *fragilis*	✓			✓	✓		✓	✓	✓						✓			
424.	**Phebalium** *squameum*	✓			✓				✓	✓	✓	✓						✓	✓
425.	Phebalium *squamulosum*	✓			✓	✓			✓	✓	✓	✓				✓			
426.	**Phyla** *nodiflora*				✓				✓	✓	✓	✓		✓					

427. **Pimelea** *ferruginea*																		
428. **Pittosporum** *rhombifolium*																		
429. Pittosporum *undulatum*																		
430. **Podocarpus** *lawrencei*																		
431. Podocarpus *elatus*																		
432. **Pomaderris** *ferruginea*																		
433. **Prostanthera** *lasianthos*																		
434. Prostanthera *ovalifolia*																		
435. **Ptilotus** *obovatus*																		
436. **Rhagodia** *nutans*																		
437. **Rhododendron** *lochae*																		
438. **Ricinocarpus** *pinifolius*																		
439. **Rulingea** *hermanifolia*																		
440. **Scaevola** *aemula*																		
441. Scaevola *albida*																		
442. Scaevola *calendulacea*																		
443. **Sollya** *heterophylla*																		
444. **Sowerbaea** *juncea*																		
445. **Spyridium** *cinereum*																		

#	Species
446.	**Stenocarpus** *sinuatus*
447.	**Stylidium** *graminifollum*
448.	**Stypandra** *glauca*
449.	**Swainsona** *galegifolia*
450.	**Syncarpia** *glomulifera*
451.	**Syzygium** *coolminianum*
452.	Syzygium *luehmanni*
453.	Syzygium *moorei*
454.	**Telopea** *speciosissima*
455.	**Thomasia** *macrocarpa*
456.	**Thomasia** *petalocalyx*
457.	**Thryptomene** *saxicola*
458.	**Thysanotus** *multiflorus*
459.	**Tristaniopsis** *laurina*
460.	**Viola** *betonicifolia*
461.	Viola *hederacea*
462.	**Westringia** *brevifolia var. 'Raleighi'*
463.	Westringia *fruticosa*
464.	Westringia *glabra*

Descriptions

Note: To be used in conjunction with the table, 'Characteristics at a glance'.

ABAREMA

Rainforest trees belonging to the same family as wattles. Often used as street trees in northern N.S.W. and Queensland. Not well known in cultivation but are deserving of more attention.

1. *ABAREMA GRANDIFLORA*

Medium size tree with glossy deep green leaves and fragrant red fluffy ball flowers followed by ornamental twisted seed pods.

2. *ABAREMA SAPINDOIDES*

Small tree with glossy deep green leaves and yellow fluffy flowers followed by attractive twisted seed pods which split open revealing shiny black seeds on a red background.

1

2

6

5

7

Purpurea form 7

ACACIA

This is a large genus of hundreds of species, a great many of which are found in cultivation. They range in size from prostrate ground covers to large stately trees. A comparatively small number are described, but many others are worthy of consideration.

Note: In the following descriptions for simplicity the foliage is referred to as 'leaves'. However, many wattles do not have true leaves (very tricky!) and the foliage is really flattened branches called 'phyllodes'.

3. *ACACIA ACINACEA*
Gold Dust Wattle

Medium shrub with narrow foliage and golden ball flowers in spring. An adaptable and hardy species.

4. *ACACIA ACULEATISSIMA*
Creeping Wattle

Small plant with thin thorn-like foliage and a profusion of fragrant solitary flowers. Excellent rockery specimen. Hardy once established.

5. *ACACIA ADUNCA*
Wallangarra Wattle

Large shrub with a profusion of golden flowers which may occur from winter to summer.

6. *ACACIA AMBLIGONA*

Variable shrub taking many forms. Popular is a prostrate form ideally suited to rockeries, pot culture and hanging baskets.

7. *ACACIA BAILEYANA*
Cootamundra Wattle

Small tree with beautiful grey fern-like foliage and profusion of golden ball flowers in late winter. Will benefit greatly by heavy pruning – up to 30% of foliage – immediately after flowering. Another form (A. baileyana purpurea) has purple foliage. An outstanding plant.

8. *ACACIA BOORMANI*
Snowy River Wattle

Outstanding medium rounded shrub, often multi-stemmed, bearing a profusion of delicate yellow ball flowers in early spring. Needs a sheltered sunny position for best results.

9. *ACACIA BUXIFOLIA*
Box-leaved Wattle

Popular medium shrub, spectacular in flower. Prefers a sheltered site and often reproduces itself.

10. *ACACIA CALAMIFOLIA*
Wallowa

Lovely rounded shrub to 3 metres, bearing bright golden yellow fragrant flowers in spring.

11. *ACACIA CARDIOPHYLLA*
Wyalong Wattle

A beautiful feathery leafed wattle with arching branches and small but bright flowers. Highly drought resistant. May lose its leaves if drainage is poor.

12. *ACACIA CULTRIFORMIS*
Knife Leaf Wattle

An upright medium shrub to 3 metres, with graceful drooping branches and unusual knife shaped leaves. A hardy specimen in most positions, and an attractive foliage plant.

13. *ACACIA DEALBATA*
Silver Wattle

Similar to A. baileyana. Will withstand cold conditions. Often reproduces from suckers.

14. *ACACIA DECORA*
Graceful Wattle

A small to medium shrub, spectacular in flower, and very drought resistant. Covered in masses of golden ball flowers in spring.

8

9

12

11

15

Ph: MWH 15

70

16

17

18

15. *ACACIA DECURRENS*
Black Wattle

A very rapid growing small tree with fine deep green foliage offset by rich golden blossom in spring. Useful as a 'pioneer' plant for quick early display and later removal. May be short lived. Useful for both coastal and inland plantings.

16. *ACACIA DRUMMONDI*
Drummond's Wattle

Very dainty small shrub from W.A. with blue-grey feathery foliage and pale yellow rod like flowers. Useful for small gardens.

17. *ACACIA ELATA*
Cedar Wattle

Very attractive small tree with deep green fern-like foliage and pale cream ball flowers in summer.

18. *ACACIA ELONGATA*
Swamp Wattle

Particularly attractive long flowering species with narrow rigid foliage and golden ball flowers in spring. Very adaptable and fairly drought resistant.

19. *ACACIA FIMBRIATA*
Fringe Wattle

Sweetly scented light yellow ball flowers in spring and narrow grey-green leaves. A large shrub suitable for moist gullies.

20. *ACACIA GLAUCESCENS*
Coastal Myall

This very attractive species is a small tree used extensively for landscaping. It has large silver-grey leaves and lemon-yellow rod like flowers in spring. Suitable for coastal and near inland areas.

21. *ACACIA GLAUCOPTERA*

A straggling prostrate shrub with blue wing-like leaves, red tipped in new growth and interspersed with golden ball flowers in spring. Requires a well drained sunny site and regular pruning.

22. *ACACIA GRACILIFOLIA*

Medium shrub with fine needle-like foliage and golden ball flowers in spring. Very graceful plant.

19

20

23

28

23. *ACACIA HOWITTI*
Sticky Wattle

A vigorously growing large dense shrub with pale green foliage. An excellent hedge or windbreak plant. Flowers are pale yellow. Foliage exudes pervasive but beautiful aroma on warm days. Requires heavy pruning immediately after flowering.

24. *ACACIA ITEAPHYLLA*
Flinders Range Wattle

Medium shrub with narrow blue-green foliage on drooping branches. Has showy yellow ball flowers bursting from unusual catkin-like buds.

22

Prostrate form   31

24

25. ACACIA *KETTLEWELLIAE*
Buffalo Wattle

Large shrub or small tree with attractive foliage and dense clusters of golden ball flowers in spring and summer. Suitable for sub-alpine areas.

26. ACACIA *LANIGERA*
Woolly Wattle

A hardy small rounded shrub with woolly new growth and small golden ball flowers in spring.

27. ACACIA *LINIFOLIA*
Flax Wattle

A medium open shrub with arching branches, narrow dark green leaves and a profusion of pale yellow flowers. A hardy shrub which may flower any time from mid-summer to mid-winter.

28. ACACIA *LONGIFOLIA*
Sydney Golden Wattle

A rapid growing medium shrub which thrives under coastal conditions. Easily the most popular acacia for landscaping in N.S.W. Long mid green leaves and delicately scented golden rod flowers in winter and spring. Adaptable to both moist and dry conditions. A good 'pioneer' plant.

29. ACACIA *LONGIFOLIA VAR. SOPHORAE*
Coastal Wattle

A form of A. longifolia having slightly broader foliage and often prostrate habit. Ideally suited to coastal planting and dune stabilization.

30. ACACIA *MEARNSI*
Green or Black Wattle

A small tree with dark green fern like foliage and cream ball shaped flowers in spring. A rapid growing and hardy species. A good 'pioneer' plant.

31. ACACIA *MELANOXYLON*
Blackwood

This is the blackwood popular for furniture manufacture. A large tree with drooping grey-green foliage, pale yellow ball flowers and attractive curved seed pods. Popular overseas. Prefers a rich, moist soil.

32. ACACIA *MYRTIFOLIA*
Myrtle Wattle

An adaptable small shrub found on a wide variety of soil types. Mid green leaves are edged with red, and stems are also red. Flowers are pale yellow, winter to summer. Will grow in the shade, but takes a more attractive form in full sun.

Ph: MWH 34
Ph: MWH 35

33. *ACACIA OXYCEDRUS*
Spike Wattle

Medium shrub with sharply pointed and rigid foliage. Worth growing for its golden yellow flower spikes in early spring.

34. *ACACIA PARRAMATTENSIS*
Green Wattle

Very similar to A. decurrens and A. Mearnsii, but has a longer life. Scented yellow flowers throughout summer.

36

39

38

40

Ph: MWH 41

Highland form 43

44

42

35. ACACIA PENDULA
Weeping Myall

Pendulous small tree with handsome grey foliage on very slender branches. Pale cream ball flowers in spring. This species is an attractive foliage plant for inland areas.

36. ACACIA PODALYRIIFOLIA
Mt. Morgan or Queensland Silver Wattle

Tall shrub or small tree wich may be short lived. Always a pleasure to see the brilliant perfumed golden flowers in mid-winter. Requires reasonable drainage.

37. ACACIA PRAVISSIMA
Ovens Wattle

Beautiful and graceful species with drooping angular branches and triangular foliage. Tall shrub bearing a profusion of golden ball flowers from bronze buds. A prostrate form now in cultivation is sold as 'Golden Carpet'.

38. ACACIA PROMINENS
Gosford Wattle or Golden Rain Tree

A small tree with dense clusters of very sweetly scented golden ball flowers which are unaffected by rain. Prefers moist soils.

39. ACACIA PYCNANTHA
Australian Golden Wattle

This wattle is featured on the Australian Coat of Arms. A medium shrub or small tree with bright green sickle shaped foliage and large golden ball flowers. Very showy, rapid growing and suitable for inland and coastal planting.

40. ACACIA SALIGNA
(Also referred to as Acacia cyanophylla)
Orange Wattle

An attractive small tree with drooping grey-green foliage and dense clusters of bright golden ball flowers in spring and summer. A rapid grower suitable for dune stabilization and coastal plantings.

41. ACACIA SPECTABILIS
Mudgee Wattle

Beautiful tall shrub with dainty soft blue foliage and golden ball flowers in spring.

42. ACACIA SUAVEOLENS
Sweet Scented Wattle

A slender upright medium shrub with thick rigid blue-green foliage and pale yellow flowers in winter and spring. Flowers are perfumed.

43. ACACIA TERMINALIS
Sunshine Wattle

Attractive but short lived medium shrub with open habit and bronze-green fernlike foliage. Pale to deep golden flowers winter and spring.

44. ACACIA UNCINATA

Small to medium shrub with weeping branches and round wavy leaves. Flowers are deep golden yellow, fragrant, and carried throughout the year.

45. *ACACIA VESTITA*
Hairy Wattle

Attractive and compact medium shrub with weeping habit, triangular leaves and grey woolly foliage. Dense clusters of golden ball flowers in spring and summer. An outstanding plant. Suitable for hedges.

46. *ACMENA SMITHI*
Lilly Pilly

A small tree with a dense crown of dark green leaves, with flowers and edible white berries tinged with purple. A reliable species.

47. *ACTINOTUS HELIANTHI*
Flannel Flower

A small upright shrub with woolly grey foliage and creamy white daisy like flowers with a flannel texture. Flowers through summer.

48. *ADENANTHOS BARBIGERUS*

A small shrub belonging to the same family as Grevilleas. It has an erect twiggy habit with pointed blue grey foliage and bright red tubular flowers. Flowers in spring.

46

47

47

51

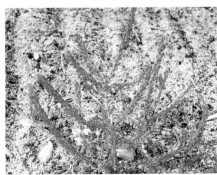

49

49. *ADENANTHOS OBOVATUS*

An upright open shrub with dull green leaves and bright red tubular flowers in winter and spring. Prefers a well drained soil.

52

54

52. *ALLOCASUARINA TORULOSA*
Forest Oak

A small to medium tree with rough corky bark. The fine green foliage, which at times turns red to purple, gives the tree a soft weeping appearance. Very hardy and adaptable.

53. *ANGOPHORA BAKERI*

An attractive small tree for poorer soils with narrow foliage and a profusion of white flowers in early summer. Rough, scaly bark.

54. *ANGOPHORA COSTATA*
Smooth Barked Apple or Red Gum

A rapid growing free flowering medium tree often assuming a gnarled habit. It has attractive salmon pink dimpled bark and a profusion of white flowers in late spring.

55. *ANGOPHORA HISPIDA*
Dwarf Apple (syn. Angophora cordifolia)

An often twisted shrub or small tree with broad, coarse stem clasping leaves and large sprays of creamy white flowers in summer. Responds well to regular fertilizing and periodic lopping.

50. *AGONIS FLEXUOSA*
Willow Myrtle

A small to medium tree with arching branches, narrow foliage and clusters of small white flowers along the branches in spring. A number of varieties are available including Agonis flexuosa 'Fairy Foliage', a dwarf form, and Agonis flexuosa 'Variegata', a form with fine, variegated foliage. Dwarf forms are suitable for tubs.

51. *AGONIS JUNIPERINA*
Native Cedar

An upright medium shrub reminiscent of a conifer with fine, dark green leaves and a profusion of white flowers throughout the year.

ANIGOZANTHOS

A family of about 8 species. With the exception of A. flavidus, most have been difficult to maintain in the Eastern States. However, hybrids are being introduced which combine the reliability of A. flavidus with the compact growth and spectacular flowering of some of the more difficult forms.

56. *ANIGOZANTHOS FLAVIDUS*
Kangaroo Paw

A clumpy plant with strap like leaves which may grow 300 mm to 1 m high. The yellow green or pink red flowers are carried on long spikes held high above the foliage in summer. A robust plant adaptable to most soils containing reasonable moisture.

57. *ANIGOZANTHOS HUMILIS*
Cat's Paw

A small species usually less than 150 mm high with sickle shaped leaves and bright orange yellow flower spikes. Difficult to maintain in cultivation.

58. *ANIGOZANTHOS MANGLESI*
Red & Green Kangaroo Paw
(W.A. floral emblem)

A showy plant with blue grey foliage to 400 mm with striking red and green flowers. Difficult to maintain, and particularly susceptible to ink disease.

59. *ANIGOZANTHOS VIRIDIS*
Green Kangaroo Paw

A small plant with rush like foliage and green flower spikes. More reliable than other small forms. Requires reasonable moisture.

Hybrid

Dwarf delight

57

58

59

58

60. ARAUCARIA BIDWILLI
Bunya Pine

A tall conifer like tree with deep green sharply pointed foliage suitable for parks and very large gardens.

61. ARAUCARIA CUNNINGHAMI
Hoop Pine

A tall tree for parks and large gardens. Similar to Norfolk Island Pine.

62. ARCHONTOPHOENIX CUNNIN-GHAMIANA
Bangalow Palm

A rapid growing palm for shady moist situations. Grows to 10 m.

63. ASTARTIA FASCICULARIS

A small heath like shrub to 1 m with fine foliage and a profusion of small white or pale pink 5-petalled flowers borne throughout the year. A hardy and reliable plant.

64. ASTARTIA HETERANTHERA

Similar to A. fascicularis, although smaller and more open.

61

65. ASTROLOMA CILIATUM

A small often prostrate plant with pale green pine-like foliage and green tipped tubular flowers contracted at the ends. Flowers winter and early spring.

66. AUSTROMYRTUS DULCIS

An ideal small shrub for shady moist soils. Leaves develop reddish tonings. White flowers are followed by small fleshy berries. Reliable.

67. AUSTROMYRTUS TENUIFOLIA

An erect medium shrub with narrow leaves, white flowers and greenish blue fleshy fruit. Prefers a moist shady site.

60

Ph: MWH 62

65

68. *BACKHOUSIA CITRIODORA*
Lemon Scented Myrtle

A small tree with dense foliage reaching to the ground and a profusion of white flowers. Crushed foliage is very aromatic.

69. *BACKHOUSIA MYRTIFOLIA*

A hardy small tree from rainforests and creek banks producing masses of small cream flowers.

70. *BAECKEA DENSIFOLIA*

A small rounded shrub with dull green leaves and small white flowers in summer. A hardy plant adapted to semi shade.

71. *BAECKEA LINIFOLIA*

An attractive pendulous shrub to 2 m with small white flowers borne throughout the year. Thrives in poorly drained soils.

64

Ph: MWH 68

Baecka astarteoides

72. *BAECKEA VIRGATA*

A variable shrub, often reaching 4 m, rather formal in appearance. Bears masses of white flowers in summer and is particular hardy. A number of dwarf forms are available, some growing less than 300 mm. Small forms are suitable for tubs.

BANKSIA

Of the more than 60 Banksia species found in Australia, less than 10 occur in the Eastern States. Generally, attempts to cultivate the many beautiful W.A. varieties in the Eastern States have been disappointing. All Banksias are showy, unusual and highly desirable specimens. They attract both honeyeating birds and mammals. Banksias provide a good display in autumn.

73

Ph: MWH 74

Ph: MWH 75

76

Ph: MWH 77

76

Ph: MWH 78

73. *BANKSIA BAUERI*
Possum Banksia

Rounded small to medium shrub with large woolly yellow grey flower spikes giving rise to the name 'Possum Banksia'. Requires a well drained sunny position. W.A. species popular in cultivation there. Has been grown with some success in the Eastern States.

74. *BANKSIA CALEYI*

Medium bushy shrub. Has interesting reddy-brown pendant spikes. W.A. species, but has been grown with some success in the Eastern States.

75. *BANKSIA COCCINEA*
Waratah Banksia

Perhaps the most striking of the Banksias, the 'Waratah Banksia' has fiery red short cylindrical spikes and is reminiscent of the N.S.W. waratah. A multi-stemmed plant which may grow to 4 metres. A W.A. species very difficult to cultivate in the East.

76. *BANKSIA ERICIFOLIA*
Heath Banksia

Believed to be the first specimen collected by Sir Joseph Banks at Botany Bay in 1770. A very well known large shrub ideally suited for landscaping. Often considered the best of the Eastern States Banksias, it makes an excellent screen.

Foliage is short and heath-like. Flower spikes may be as long as 40 cm and are bright orange fading to brown. A number of cultivars are available, including 'Giant Candles'. Very hardy.

77. *BANKSIA GRANDIS*
Bull or Giant Banksia

Large shrub to small tree, this upright species features very large bright yellow flower spikes. A W.A. species which has had some success in the East. Full sun and good drainage are essential.

78. *BANKSIA HOOKERANA*
Hooker's Banksia

A particularly ornamental species growing to 3 metres with long narrow serrated foliage and large woolly flower spikes which change from light to deep golden yellow as the flower matures. A rapid grower used extensively for cut flowers. A W.A. species not suited to the Eastern States.

79. *BANKSIA INTEGRIFOLIA*
Coast Banksia

This small tree from the coastal regions of the Eastern States is easily grown and very hardy and produces an abundance of yellow flower spikes in autumn.

80. *BANKSIA MARGINATA*
Silver Banksia

Similar to B. integrifolia. Adapts well to garden conditions.

81. *BANKSIA MEDIA*

The easiest W.A. Banksia to cultivate in the East. Compact, medium shrub producing yellow rather formal 'corn cob' flower spikes. Resistant to salt spray.

82. *BANKSIA PETIOLARIS*

One of a number of prostrate Banksias, producing flower spikes from branches growing at or below ground level. Flower spikes are yellow. A W.A. species requiring excellent drainage which has had some success in the East.

83. *BANKSIA PROSTRATA*
Prostrate Banksia

Similar to B. petiolaris, but has brown flower spikes. W.A. Species. Some success in the East.

79

79

80

Ph: MWH 81

Ph: MWH 84

Ph: CHS 86

87

Ph: MWH 83

Ph: MWH 85

85. *BANKSIA ROBUR*
Swamp or Broad Leafed Banksia

A fascinating Eastern States Banksia, with large wavy and leathery leaves. The younger branches and leaves are covered with velvety brown hairs. A hardy medium shrub producing flower spikes with change from bluish-green through yellow-green tipped with black to reddish-brown.

86. *BANKSIA SERRATA*
Saw Banksia

This is the 'Old Man' Banksia, a crooked and gnarled tree with a thick, short trunk and low spreading twisted branches. Leaves are bright green and evenly serrated. Flower spikes are an attractive silvery gold, greying with age. Small Eastern States tree. A beautiful garden specimen. Also excellent in large pots.

87. *BANKSIA SERRATIFOLIA*
(syn. Banksia aemula)
Wallum Banksia

Very similar to B. serrata but not quite as large.

84. *BANKSIA REPENS*
Creeping Banksia

A feature of this Banksia is the deeply divided foliage which, like the other prostrate Banksias (B. petiolaris and B. prostrata) is stiff and erect. Flower spikes are an attractive tan brown. W.A. species. Some success in the East.

88

88. *BANKSIA SPINULOSA*
Hairpin Banksia

A variable medium shrub. The golden spike appears to support an array of purple hairpins. This eastern species is easy to cultivate and will tolerate poor soils.

88

89

Ph: MWH 94

90

Ph: MWH 95

Ph: CHS 93

89. BAUERA RUBIOIDES
Dog or River Rose

A broad straggly shrub to 1 m suitable for sun or shade bearing masses of rose pink flowers. Reliable if given ample moisture. White flowered forms are also attractive.

90. BAUERA SESSILIFLORA

More upright than B. rubioides and having showy mauve pink flowers growing close to the stems.

91. BEAUFORTIA MACROSTEMON

A much branched small shrub with small grey leaves and attractive red and yellow bottle brush flowers in spring. A drought resistant hardy species.

92. BEAUFORTIA SPARSA

An erect shrub with fine foliage and red bottle brush flowers in late summer. Suitable for well drained sites with ample moisture.

93. BILLARDIERA SCANDENS
Apple Berry

An open climbing plant bearing creamy yellow tubular flowers and fleshy edible fruit. A hardy small climber for sun and shade.

94. BLANDFORDIA GRANDIFLORA
Christmas Bell

Stiff deep green grass like leaves to 500 mm with large pendulous orange to red ball flowers tipped with yellow. Needs ample moisture for rapid growth. May take 2 or 3 years to reach flowering age.

95. BLANDFORDIA PUNICEA
Christmas Bell

Similar to B. grandiflora. Brush like foliage with yellow throated red bell flowers.

96. BORONIA ANEMONIFOLIA

A small upright shrub with fine foliage bearing small pink buds and white flowers throughout the year. An excellent rockery or tub plant.

97. BORONIA DENTICULATA

An upright shrub to 1 m with blue green narrow foliage and pink star flowers in spring. A moderately hardy species.

98. BORONIA FLORIBUNDA

An upright shrub with pale green ferny foliage and an abundance of soft pink flowers with a delicate fragrance. Very showy, but requires excellent drainage.

99. BORONIA HETEROPHYLLA

A dense rounded shrub with fine deep green foliage and bearing masses of deep pink bell like flowers in spring. May be difficult to maintain.

Plant in full bud   96

Ph: MWH   97

Yellow form   101

100

101

103

105

104

100. BORONIA LEDIFOLIA

Sydney Boronia

An open shrub to 1 m usually with 3 lobed foliage bearing showy pink flowers in spring. White and multi petalled varieties are sometimes encountered. Difficult to maintain.

101. BORONIA MEGASTIGMA

Brown Boronia

A fine foliage plant to 1 m or more bearing masses of yellow throated brown flowers prized for their fragrance. Other flower forms include all yellow and burgundy with yellow. Light pruning after flowering prolongs life. Sparing applications of fertilizer are beneficial.

102. BORONIA MOLLOYAE

A compact shrub to 1.5 m with aromatic soft green foliage and pink flowers in spring. Moderately hardy.

103. BORONIA MUELLERI

The 'Sunset Serenade' cultivar of this boronia is an attractive small shrub with delicate pink star flowers. A reasonably hardy and recommended species.

104. BORONIA PINNATA

A variable shrub to 1.5 m with fragrant ferny foliage and white or, more commonly, pink star flowers. Adaptable to a wide range of soil conditions.

105. BORONIA SERRULATA

A small bushy shrub to 1 m with closely packed bright green foliage and rich pink highly perfumed cup-like flowers borne in terminal clusters during spring. Highly desirable but difficult to maintain.

106. BORONIA SPATHULATA

A small shrub to 600 mm with fine oval foliage and pink starlike flowers on long arching branches.

107. *BRACHYCHITON ACERIFOLIUS*
Illawara Flame Tree

A tall semi deciduous tree with handsome bright green foliage and a profusion of red bell flowers in summer. May drop leaves during the flowering period. An adaptable and hardy species. A useful indoor plant when young.

108. *BRACHYCHITON DISCOLOR*
Lace Bark Tree

A large deciduous tree with deeply lobed foliage with a silvery underside and large pink bell flowers in summer. May drop leaves during the flowering period. Suited to most soil types.

109. *BRACHYCHITON RUPESTRE*
Bottle Tree

A medium tree whose trunk swells giving rise to its common name. Interesting juvenile foliage makes the plant an ideal indoor specimen which may be kept small by limiting root growth by planting in a small pot.

Ph: MWH   107

Ph: MWH   109

Ph: MWH   107

110

111

112

113

110. BRACHYCOME MULTIFIDA

A well know compact suckering plant to 400 mm with much divided ferny foliage and pale mauve daisy flowers throughout spring and summer.

111. BRACHYCOME SP.

Similar to B. multifida but much more compact, rarely exceeding 50 mm in height.

112. BRACHYCOME SP. 'PILLIGA' (AFFIN. MELANOCARPA)

Broad purplish green lobed foliage seldom exceeding 50 mm in height. Carries bright mauve pink daisy flowers above the foliage.

113. BRACHYSEMA LANCEOLATUM
Swan River Pea

A neat rounded shrub to 1.5 m with silver grey wavy foliage and bright red pea flowers in summer. A drought resistant species responding well to pruning.

114. BRACHYSEMA LATIFOLIUM

A prostrate or trailing plant with rounded mid green leaves and orange pea flowers. Requires good drainage.

115. BUCKINGHAMIA CELSISSIMA
Ivory Curl

A small handsome tree with dense foliage producing masses of cream flower spikes up to 200 mm long during summer. A hardy plant requiring a warm climate and reasonable moisture.

116. BURSARIA SPINOSA
Blackthorn or Tasmanian Christmas Bush

A variable erect thorny shrub with small dark green foliage and masses of fragrant white flowers during late spring and summer. Very hardy and widespread.

CALLISTEMON

This is a group of about 25 species and a large number of varieties. Most are hardy plants adaptable to a wide range of soil conditions including poorly drained soils. Most enjoy full sun, however, some will survive in shaded conditions. All are attractive to birds.

Many produce brightly coloured new foliage in colours such as pink or bronze. Crushed foliage is often fragrant.

Callistemons have the typical 'bottle brush' flower varying in colour from white to cream, yellow, green, mauve, pink, purple, carmine and bright red. Flower colour is often further highlighted by a liberal dusting of golden pollen. Pruning after flowering produces more compact growth and increases the number of flower spikes the following year.

The ease with which callistemons hybridize has led to a number of worthwhile varieties, some of which are included here.

118

119

123

Ph: MWH   122

120. *CALLISTEMON CITRINUS* 'ANZAC'

A low sprawling shrub, approximately 1 m x 3 m with large white bottle brush flowers, often tinged with pink. Flowers November to January.

121. *CALLISTEMON CITRINUS* 'AUSTRAFLORA FIREBAND'

A sprawling shrub to 2 m with arching branches and a profusion of red flower spikes. New growth is silvery pink. Flowers October to December.

122. *CALLISTEMON CITRINUS* 'ENDEAVOUR'

A dense rounded shrub of 3 m or more with dark green rigid leaves. When in flower this shrub is covered with large brilliant scarlet bottle brush flowers. Flowering may occur numerous times each year.

123. *CALLISTEMON* 'HARKNESS'

A dense rounded shrub to 3 m producing some of the largest of all bottle brush flowers. The deep red flower spikes may be more than 200 mm long. Flowers late spring and autumn. A very showy and hardy species.

117. *CALLISTEMON* 'BURGUNDY'

A medium shrub to 3 m with deep burgundy flower spikes dusted with gold. Flowers November to February.

118. *CALLISTEMON* 'CANDY PINK'

A medium shrub 2 m or more high, with dark green pointed rigid foliage and masses of pink to pale red rather open bottle brush flowers. Flowering may occur numerous times throughout the year.

119. *CALLISTEMON CITRINUS*

A rather rigid upright shrub to 4 m producing numerous red flower spikes in late spring and autumn. White flowered forms are also known. A very hardy species which responds well to fertilizer.

124. CALLISTEMON 'KINGS PARK SPECIAL'

A medium shrub to 3 m with narrow foliage and bright red terminal clusters of bottle brush flowers on arching branches. Main flowering period is December to January.

125. CALLISTEMON 'LILACINUS'

A tall shrub or small tree with attractive light purple flower spikes borne in profusion from November to February.

126. CALLISTEMON 'MAUVE MIST'

A dense rounded shrub 2 m-3 m high with silvery new growth and an abundance of large mauve gold dusted flower spikes in dense terminal clusters. Flowers fade with age. Flowers late spring.

127. CALLISTEMON PALLIDUS

An upright medium shrub with creamy yellow flower spikes from September to January. An excellent plant for waterlogged sites. Some selected forms are now in cultivation.

128. CALLISTEMON PALUDOSUS

A small tree with fine pendulous foliage and silvery pink new growth and creamy yellow bottle brush flowers. Flowers in summer.

129. CALLISTEMON PINIFOLIUS

A rather straggly spreading shrub which responds well to pruning. Usually about 2 m in height two flower forms are popular, a red and a yellow-green. Both forms feature fine pine-like but rigid foliage. A particularly hardy species well adapted to poor soils and should be more widely planted. Flowers spring and early summer.

130. CALLISTEMON POLANDI

A medium to tall shrub with stiff light green leaves and large orange red bottle brush flowers dusted with gold. New growth is often silvery pink. An attractive semi-prostrate in cultivation and is often less than 1 m in height. Both varieties of this early flowering species may be frost tender.

131. CALLISTEMON 'REEVES PINK'

An excellent small to medium shrub which produces a profusion of gold tipped pink flowers which fade with age. Responds well to pruning and makes an ideal low hedge. Flowers spring and autumn.

132. CALLISTEMON SIEBERI

A variable shrub which may reach 2 m. A good form occurring in high altitudes rarely exceeds 1 m. It has dark green narrow leaves and creamy yellow flower spikes in summer.

125

127

Ph: MWH 129

Ph: MWH 130

133

133. *CALLISTEMON SPECIOSUS*

Grows to 2 m and bears bottle brush flowers with deep red stamens and golden anthers. Although this plant is found often growing in water, it will thrive also in drier locations. Flowers spring and summer.

134. *CALLISTEMON SUBULATUS*

A small much branched shrub with narrow rigid and often sharp pointed leaves and bright red flower spikes on arching branches. Suitable for either wet or dry locations. Flowers November to February.

135. *CALLISTEMON 'TINAROO'*

A medium shrub bearing large clusters of red flowers tipped with gold. The dark green often crowded foliage may be bronze in new growth. Flowers in spring.

136. *CALLISTEMON VIMINALIS*

A variable shrub or small tree ranging from less than 1 m to more than 12 m in height. Usually has a weeping habit, pale green foliage, and a profusion of bright red flower spikes suitable for cutting. Grown from seed, the plant varies considerably and descriptions of a number of better forms follow.

137. *CALLISTEMON VIMINALIS 'CAPTAIN COOK'*

A well known dwarf form reaching a height of 2 m. Dense clusters of red bottle brush flowers are borne on the ends of the branches in spring, autumn and possibly other times during the year.

138. *CALLISTEMON VIMINALIS 'DAWSON RIVER'*

Tall shrub or small tree with long weeping branches and large crimson flower spikes and golden yellow anthers. Flowers in spring.

139. *CALLISTEMON VIMINALIS 'HANNAH RAY'*

A small tree with long weeping branches, large crimson brushes and pink new growth. An ideal street tree. Spring flowering.

140. *CALLISTEMON VIMINALIS 'HEN CAMP CREEK'*

A medium shrub with broad bluish green new foliage and bright red brushes in spring and autumn.

141. *CALLISTEMON VIMINALIS 'PROLIFIC'*

An upright small tree with bright green foliage and large clusters of deep red bottle brush flowers late winter to early spring.

136

Ph: MWH 135

Ph: MWH 139

142. CALLISTEMON VIMINALIS 'RUNNING RIVER'

A dense dwarf shrub having soft hairy foliage, bronze in new growth and large clusters of deep red rather open flower spikes. Flowers in spring.

143. CALLISTEMON 'WESTERN GLORY'

An upright medium shrub with sharp pointed leathery leaves and terminal clusters of mauve red flower spikes in late spring.

144. CALLISTEMON 'BAROONDAH'

A medium shrub with long weeping branches and silvery new growth and masses of pale pink bottle brush flowers in terminal clusters. Deserves to be more popular. Flowers in spring.

145. CALLISTEMON SPECIES 'INJUNE'

Small to medium shrub with silky pink new growth and pale pink or red flower spikes produced in several flushes throughout the year. The flowers fade with age to produce a variety of colours on the one plant.

149

Ph: MWH   150

150

146. CALLITRIS ENDLICHERI
Black Cypress Pine

An upright conical small tree with fine green foliage and generally formal appearance. Drought resistant.

147. CALLITRIS HUGELI
White Cypress Pine

Medium to tall tree with conical upright shape and blue green foliage. Hardy.

148. CALLITRIS MACLEAYANA

An upright medium tree with columnar habit and dark green foliage, often colouring in winter. A rainforest species adapting well to full sun.

Ph: MWH   151

152

153

Ph: MWH   154

155

154

149. CALLITRIS RHOMBOIDEA
Port Jackson Pine

An upright tree to 15 m with green or blue foliage, slightly pendulous. Very attractive and hardy species. Ideal for coastal plantings.

150. CALOCEPHALUS BROWNI

A small rounded wiry shrub with a very silvery appearance bearing insignificant pale yellow flowers. An excellent foliage plant requiring regular pruning to maintain habit. Resistant to salt spray.

151. CALOTHAMNUS QUADRIFIDUS

An upright spreading shrub to 2 m with attractive narrow pine like foliage with long soft flower spikes resembling a one sided bottle brush. Flowers are red, occasionally yellow in winter and spring. Very hardy drought resistant shrub.

152. CALOTHAMNUS VILLOSUS
Woolly Net Bush

An upright rounded shrub to 2 m with soft grey foliage covered with fine silvery hairs. Bright red one sided flower spikes during winter, spring and summer. A hardy shrub.

153. CALYTRIX SULLIVANI
Fringe Myrtle

A small shrub to 1 m with fine heath like foliage and soft pink flowers. Good drainage is required.

154. CALYTRIX TETRAGONA
Fringe Myrtle

A variable but dense plant ranging up to 1.5 m. The fine heathlike foliage is bright green with white star like flowers.

155. CARPOBROTUS GLAUCESCENS
Angular Pig Face

A creeping plant with long triangular greyish green fleshy leaves and large bright mauve pink daisy flowers with yellow centre. Excellent for dune stabilization and beach front plantings.

156. CASSIA ACIPHYLLA
Cassia

A low spreading shrub usually less than 1 m with dark green divided foliage and large bright yellow buttercup flowers. Suitable for most soil types.

157. CASSIA ARTEMISOIDES
Silver Cassia

A beautiful rounded shrub to 2 m with finely divided blue grey foliage and dainty bright yellow buttercup flowers followed by dark seed pods with a varnished appearance. Both flowers and pods are carried for a long period. Will tolerate most soil types.

158. CASUARINA CUNNINGHAMIANA
River Oak

A very useful medium tree to 20 m with fine slightly pendulous foliage suitable for both coastal and inland plantings.

159. CASUARINA GLAUCA
Swamp Oak

A rounded often open medium tree with coarse slightly pendulous foliage which 'sings' in the wind. A very hardy species which tolerates wet soils.

160. CASUARINA NANA
Dwarf Oak

A much branched low spreading shrub with fine dark green foliage providing an excellent ground cover or low wind break for exposed and coastal situations.

161. CASUARINA STRICTA
Drooping She Oak

An attractive rounded small tree to 10 m with long pendulous branchlets. A salt resistant tree suitable for most soils.

162. CERATOPETALUM GUMMIFERUM
N.S.W. Christmas Bush

A well known upright shrub to 5 m with pale green trifoliate leaves, white star flowers followed by showy reddy calyces giving the tree an overall pink appearance. Excellent for cut flowers. Prefers good drainage.

163. CHAMELAUCIUM UNCINATUM
Geraldton Wax

An open spreading shrub to 3 m with fine foliage and large waxy 5-petalled flowers which may vary from white to deep purple. Pink forms are most common. Requires protected well drained sunny position.

157

157

158

159

Ph: MWH   162

Red form   Ph: MWH   163

164

164

Ph: MWH   165

166

Ph: MWH   166

164. *CHORIZEMA CORDATUM*
Flame Pea

A low bushy shrub with bright green heart shaped leaves which bear a profusion of bright orange and yellow pea flowers in spring. A spectacular long flowering shrub.

165. *CLEMATIS ARISTATA*
Clematis

A vigorous climbing plant with pale green foliage bearing silvery white markings producing a profusion of creamy white flowers followed by feathery fruit equally as showy as the flower. A hardy plant requiring reasonable moisture.

166. *CONOSTYLUS ACULEATA*

A small clump plant to 300 mm with long strap like leaves and woolly yellow flowers held above the foliage.

167. CORREA ALBA

A rounded shrub which may reach 1.5 m with attractive round greeny grey foliage and white star like flowers. Requires well drained soil. Resistant to salt spray.

168. CORREA DECUMBENS

A low spreading shrub with attractive tubular flowers red with yellow tips and dull green narrow foliage. Full sun or semi-shade.

169. CORREA PULCHELLA

A variable shrub with orange to pink bell shaped flowers responsible for a number of varieties of hybrids, some of the best being Correa manni and Correa 'Dusky Bells'.

Pink flowered form   167

170

170. CORREA REFLEXA

A variable shrub ranging from 300 mm to 1.5 m with bell shaped flowers ranging from greenish yellow to deep red.

171. CROWEA EXALATA

A rounded shrub with fine foliage and bright pink star flowers. A moderately hardy plant suitable for full sun or semi-shade. Flowers autumn and winter.

172. CROWEA SALIGNA

A small rounded shrub with bright green foliage and unusual angular branches. Large deep pink star-like flowers appear in autumn and winter. An outstanding shrub for light shade. Difficult to maintain. Suitable for cut flowers.

Ph: MWH   172

174

Ph: MWH 176

178

173

173. CUPANIOPSIS ANACARDIOIDES
Tuckeroo

A rapid growing small to medium tree with glossy green large fern like leaves. The small flowers are followed by showy black seeds. An ideal tree for salt laden winds.

174. DAMPIERA DIVERSIFOLIA

A vigorously growing prostrate plant which suckers as it spreads and produces masses of dark blue flowers over a long period. Requires a well drained soil with ample moisture. Ideal for rockeries, tubs and baskets.

175. DAMPIERA SERICANTHA

A free flowering low suckering plant with pale ivy-like foliage and bright blue flowers year round. A hardy species, ideal for rockeries.

176. DARWINIA CITRIODORA
Lemon-scented Myrtle

A compact bushy shrub to 1 m with pale blue grey lemon scented foliage and small yellow and red flowers. Attractive to birds and tolerates salt spray.

177. DIANELLA TASMANICA

A clumpy plant with strappy flax-like leaves and long spikes of bright blue flowers with yellow anthers. An ideal contrast plant, especially near water gardens.

178. DILLWYNIA FLORIBUNDA
Egg & Bacon

An open shrub to 1 m with fine foliage and masses of golden yellow pea flowers during late winter and early spring. Often short lived.

179. DIPLARRENA MORAEA

An upright clump plant with glossy green strappy leaves and white iris-like flowers with a yellow centre. A hardy plant.

180. DODONAEA VISCOSA
Hop Bush

A bushy shrub to 3 m with leaves having a sticky texture, small flowers and green three winged fruit. This is an excellent and hardy foliage plant suitable for hedges and windbreaks with foliage suitable for cutting. Both green and purple foliage forms are available.

181. DORYANTHES EXCELSA
Gymea Lily

A striking contrast plant. Large sword shaped leaves to 1 m, and huge red flower heads on long stalks some metres above the foliage. A large hardy plant which may take some years to flower.

182. DRYANDRA POLYCEPHALA

I have included this shrub as Dryandras are too spectacular to ignore. However, they have been difficult to maintain in the Eastern States. This species is a shrub to 3 m with saw toothed leaves and bright yellow flower heads.

183. ELEOCARPUS RETICULATUS
Blueberry Ash

A small upright tree with dark green glossy leaves. White flowers are followed by dark blue berries which attract birds. Suitable to most soils. An attractive pink flowered form is available.

181

184. EPACRIS IMPRESSA
Common Heath (Victorian Floral Emblem)

A straggly small shrub with small stem-clasping foliage and showy tubular flowers in white pink or red at various times during the year. Need a well drained moist site.

185. EPACRIS LONGIFLORA

A small shrub with long straggly branches and short deep green stem-clasping leaves which produces long rows of pendulous red tubular flowers tipped with white. Prefers a shady, moist but well drained site.

186. EREMOPHILA GIBIFOLIA

A small open shrub with tiny leaves and small purple flowers. A reasonable hardy species suitable for rockeries and small gardens.

Ph: MWH   181

Pink form   Ph: MWH   183

Ph: MWH   182

White form   184

185

187

187. *EREMOPHILA GLABRA*
Emu Bush

A shrub of considerable variation, often growing to 1.5 m with green or blue-grey foliage and interesting tubular flowers. Flowers may be pale-green, yellow or red. There is an attractive prostrate form with yellow flowers.

Double flowered form   191

Ph: MWH   188

190

188. *EREMOPHILA MACULATA*
Spotted Emu Bush

Probably the best known eremophila, with pale green foliage and orange tubular flowers with spotted throats. A reliable and hardy shrub common in cultivation.

189. *EREMOPHILA POLYCLADA*

A scrambling medium shrub, often less than 1 m high, with narrow bright green leaves and large showy white flowers with spotted throats. Quite a hardy plant deserving of more attention.

190. *ERIOSTEMON MYOPOROIDES*
Native Daphne

A shrub whose leaf, flower and overall size may vary considerably. Leaves range from short and rounded to very long and narrow. Flowers may be small and produced in abundance or larger and fewer in number. Most common forms range from 1 to 2 m, but larger forms are available. This shrub has adapted well to cultivation and is suited to a wide range of soil types in sun or partial shade. Responds well to pruning. Highly recommended.

191. *ERIOSTEMON VERRUCOSUS*

A reasonably hardy species with small rounded foliage and white flowers opening from pink buds. Some very showy 'double' flowered forms are available.

EUCALYPTUS

There are some 600 species of Eucalyptus, and one of these will satisfy almost any particular need for a tree. Species vary from low shrubby plants to very large and majestic trees. Eucalyptus species are generally very adaptable, and one of their interesting features is that they are grown readily from seed, which is easy to collect.

Included here are those species which are suitable for the home garden in terms of size, shape, flowers, general appearance and ease of growing and maintenance.

Some species are notable for their flowers, others for their foliage. Others feature very attractive bark.

192. EUCALYPTUS ACACIIFORMIS
Wattle Leaved Peppermint

A small dense spreading tree suitable for a wide range of soil types. Has fine blue green foliage and small white flowers. Often sold as E. nicholi to which it is very similar.

193. EUCALYPTUS ALPINA
Grampians Gum

A low spreading tree with twisted branches and coarse leaves popular in cooler climates such as Canberra and Melbourne. Very hardy.

192

194. EUCALYPTUS BOTRYOIDES
Bangalay

A tree to 20 m with rough fibrous bark. Frost hardy and will tolerate saline soils. A small form known as E. botryoides nana is available.

195. EUCALYPTUS CAESIA
Gungurru

An open tree to 8 m with blue-grey foliage and young branches and large red flowers opening from blue buds. Older brown bark peels away revealing pale green bark below. A weeping form and a large flowered form known as 'Silver

194

104

Weeping form Ph: MWH 195

Princess' are both in cultivation. Requires good drainage and low humidity.

196

197

198

199

196. *EUCALYPTUS CALOPHYLLA*
Marri

A large tree to 20 m with fibrous bark which bears a good display of cream, pink or red flowers in large clusters. Has performed well on the East Coast.

197. *EUCALYPTUS CAMALDULENSIS*
River Red Gum

A large spreading tree suitable for parks and large gardens. Has smooth white bark and grey green leaves. Will withstand long periods of inundation.

198. *EUCALYPTUS CINEREA*
Argyle Apple

A medium tree to 12 m. Young plants feature brown fibrous bark and attractive rounded blue foliage. These characteristics remain for some time and may be maintained by lopping. It is an excellent hardy specimen. Mature plants develop very dark and deeply furrowed bark and long narrow leaves. Worth planting for its foliage.

199. *EUCALYPTUS CITRIODORA*
Lemon Scented Gum

A rapid growing large often straight tree to 30 m with attractive smooth pale green to white bark and open canopy. Long soft green leaves are aromatic. Small white flowers appear in winter.

200. EUCALYPTUS CLADOCALYX NANA
Sugar Gum

A small very hardy and rapid growing tree to 10 m adaptable to a wide range of soil conditions. Branched to ground level in exposed situations.

201. EUCALYPTUS CRENULATA
Silver Gum

A small tree to 10 m with attractive grey toothed foliage ideal for cutting.

202. EUCALYPTUS CURTISI
Plunkett Mallee

A tree to 7 m ideal for small gardens, producing an abundance of cream flowers popular with birds. Adaptable to a wide range of soil conditions and frost hardy.

203. EUCALYPTUS ELATA
River Peppermint

A graceful and ornamental medium tree to 30 m with long narrow pendulous leaves and smooth white bark. White flowers are showy.

204. EUCALYPTUS EREMOPHILA
Tall Sand Mallee

Small tree to 8 m bearing masses of yellow flowers opening from long buds. A red flowered form may be available. Not recommended for the East Coast.

200

205. EUCALYPTUS ERYTHROCORYS
Illyare

A very showy small tree bearing a profusion of yellow flowers from red buds. Suitable only for drier areas.

206. EUCALYPTUS FICIFOLIA
Red Flowering Gum

A variable small tree with fibrous bark and large showy flowers followed by large urn shaped fruit. Flowers vary from whites through pinks to reds and orange. Desired colour forms are obtained by cloning and plants produced this way will be available soon.

203

Ph: MWH 205

203

Ph: MWH 207

206

208

207. *EUCALYPTUS FORRESTIANA*
Fuchsia Gum

This is a very attractive small tree bearing large red angular buds and yellow flowers. Ideal for southern and inland plantings. Less successful in the northeast.

208. *EUCALYPTUS GLOBULUS*
Tasmanian Blue Gum

Medium to large tree with broad blue juvenile foliage and semi-fibrous bark. Mature leaves are long and sickle shaped.

209. *EUCALYPTUS GLOBULUS VAR. BICOSTATA*

Similar to E. globulus but in some areas less susceptible to insect attack.

210. *EUCALYPTUS GRANDIS*
Rose or Flooded Gum

A very rapid growing tall straight tree with a handsome crown. Bark is smooth and white and scaly at the butt. May drop branches.

211. *EUCALYPTUS GROSSA*
Phillips River Gum

A small tree to 3 m with thick broad leaves on red stems. Produces an abundance of creamy yellow flowers in spring. Not suited to the East Coast.

212. *EUCALYPTUS GUMMIFERA*
Bloodwood

A large tree to 30 m with 'alligator' bark with a dense crown of shining green leaves and large clusters of white flowers irresistible to lorikeets.

213. *EUCALYPTUS GUNNI*
Cider Gum

A tall tree with pale smooth bark. Ideal for colder climates.

209

210

211

212

214

218

216

218

219

217

214. *EUCALYPTUS HAEMASTOMA*
Scribbly Gum

A small to medium tree with smooth white bark characteristically covered with a scribbly pattern left by a moth larva. An attractive tree with an open crown.

215. *EUCALYPTUS LEHMANNI*
Bushy Yate

Small rounded tree bearing large clusters of greenish yellow flowers from buds which are fused together. One of the best yellow flowered species for the East Coast. Suitable for coastal planting.

216. *EUCALYPTUS LEUCOXYLON VAR. MACROCARPA*
Whitewood

A small to medium tree with pendulous clusters of red, pink or white flowers and narrow green leaves. The best red flowering gum for the East Coast.

217. *EUCALYPTUS MACROCARPA*
Mottlecah or Rose of the West

An open straggling shrub to grow only for the challenge. Natural stands carry the largest of all eucalypt flowers being bright red and up to 125 mm across. Foliage and stems are powder blue. Difficult to establish.

218. *EUCALYPTUS MACULATA*
Spotted Gum

A tall straight tree with grey-green bark attractively dimpled and spotted with brown flakes of old bark.

219. *EUCALYPTUS MANNIFERA SUB. SP. MACULOSA*
Brittle Gum

A medium tree with pendulous blue-green foliage and attractive smooth white trunk. A very desirable species.

220. *EUCALYPTUS MICROCORYS*
Tallow Wood

A fast growing tall straight and low branching tree with fibrous bark and a dense canopy of small dark green wavy leaves.

221. *EUCALYPTUS NICHOLI*
Willow Leafed Peppermint

A graceful small tree with narrow pendulous foliage and fibrous bark. Leaves often carry a purple hue in the colder months. One of the best known and most popular garden trees.

222. *EUCALYPTUS OBTUSIFLORA*
Port Jackson Mallee

A hardy small tree to 5 m, often multi-stemmed. Has smooth greenish to pale blue stems, with bark peeling in narrow ribbons. Has thick dull green leaves and showy sprays of creamy white flowers winter and spring.

220

221

224

223. *EUCALYPTUS ORBIFOLIA*
Round Leaved Mallee

An often multi-stemmed small tree to 5 m with rounded grey green leaves. Pale blue foliage and masses of creamy white flowers. Small stems are silvery blue. Older stems are covered with a red, flakey bark. A good hardy small tree.

224. *EUCALYPTUS PAPUANA*
Ghost Gum

An attractive tree to 10 m with smooth pure white bark and glaucous foliage suitable for warm drier climates.

Ph: MWH   223

Ph: MWH   227

Ph: MWH   231

231

.ORA

th smooth
vith deeper
habit and
: for colder

'S

227. *EUCALYPTUS PTYCHOCARPA*
Swamp Bloodwood

Medium straggling tree bearing very large flowers and long broad leathery leaves. Flowers vary from white through pink to red and orange. A showy plant for warmer climates.

228. *EUCALYPTUS ROBUSTA*
Swamp Mahogany

A rapid growing medium tree to 15 m with coarse dark fibrous bark and large dark green glossy leaves. Produces an abundance of fragrant white flowers. A popular landscaping tree. Will withstand inundation.

229. *EUCALYPTUS SALIGNA*
Sydney Blue Gum

A rapid growing tall and straight tree with smooth bluey-grey bark. Needs a large garden with reasonable supply of moisture.

230. *EUCALYPTUS SCOPARIA*
Wallangarra White Gum or Willow Gum

This medium slender tree is very rapid growing in its early years. It has a clean white trunk and narrow pendulous blue green foliage. A very attractive and popular landscape tree.

231. *EUCALYPTUS SIDEROXYLON ROSEA*
Red Flowering Iron Bark

A rather slow growing medium tree with dark deeply furrowed bark and blue grey foliage. Flowers are pale to deep pink. A hardy tree for coastal or inland planting. An excellent bird attracting tree.

232. *EUCALYPTUS SPATHULATA*
Swamp Mallet

A small tree to 6 m with smooth brown polished bark, fine blue grey foliage and small white flowers.

233. *EUCALYPTUS STEEDMANI*

A small tree to 6 m with dense grey green foliage and yellow or red flowers. Suitable for drier districts.

230

A small tree with dense rounded crown and green flower clusters opening from long finger buds. A useful tree for small gardens.

234. *EUCALYPTUS TERETICORNUS*
Forest Red Gum

A very useful medium to large tree for poorer soils. It can be found on gravelly and clay soils and damp low lying ground. Has a characteristic slatey bark and upright habit.

235. *EUCALYPTUS TETRAPTERA*
Square Fruited Mallee

A desirable small tree for drier climates with unique large 4-winged buds. From these striking red buds burst pink flowers.

236. *EUCALYPTUS TORQUATA*
Coral Gum

A rapid growing attractive small tree suitable for drier climates. Carries a profusion of dainty pink flowers.

234

237. *EUCALYPTUS VIMINALIS*
Ribbon or Manna Gum

An excellent tree for large gardens and parks, with smooth bark shedding in long ribbons and white flowers throughout the year. A favourite with koalas.

238. *EUGENIA WILSONI*

A rounded often spreading shrub which may reach a diameter of 2 m. Ideal for large containers. Robust foliage with red new leaves and large very showy deep red flowers. An excellent plant.

Ph: MWH 235

239

Ph: MWH   238

239. EUTAXIA CUNEATA

A handsome small shrub and showy yellow and orange pea flowers.

Ph: MWH   238

242

240. EUTAXIA OBOVATA

A small rounded shrub to 1 m with golden yellow pea flowers in spring. Reliable in cultivation.

241. GOODENIA HEDERACEA

An attractive trailing plant which roots as it spreads with interesting rounded foliage and bright yellow flowers. A long flowering hardy plant preferring some shade.

242. GOODIA LOTIFOLIA

A vigorous plant which may reach 2 m. It has pale green trifoliate leaves and bears a profusion of bright yellow flowers in spring. A very rapid grower which seeds freely.

GREVILLEA

Have you read the Chapter on Grevilleas yet? If not, now is a good time to do so. It will give you good background on this fascinating genus.

Of the many Grevilleas from which to choose, some have adapted well to cultivation, but others have proven more difficult. Recently, some success has been achieved by grafting difficult species onto more hardy rootstock. Some grafted forms are now available. Some of the more reliable and better known species are listed.

243. GREVILLEA ACANTHIFOLIA

Spreading shrub which ranges from prostrate to 3 m. Has very prickly foliage and pink toothbrush flowers throughout the summer months. Hardy and can be used in moist and even shady conditions.

244. GREVILLEA ALPINA

Probably the most variable of all Grevilleas both in habit and colour. It is a shrub usually less than 1 m with spider flowers of red, pink, yellow or yellow-orange. Flowers throughout the year.

245. GREVILLEA AQUIFOLIUM

Very hardy small shrub with green and red toothbrush flowers and prickly holly-like leaves. Flowers winter to spring.

Ph: MWH   244

244

Red form   250

245

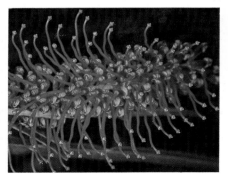

247

246. GREVILLEA ARENARIA

An excellent foliage plant with green woolly leaves which may grow to 2 m but is often smaller. Flowers may be red and green or yellow and green.

247. GREVILLEA ASPLENIFOLIA

A hardy spreading shrub to 3 m with attractive foliage and a rather formal general appearance. Cerise coloured toothbrush flowers suitable for cutting. Flowers winter and spring.

248. GREVILLEA 'AUSTRAFLORA CANTERBURY GOLD'

Low growing hardy plant with pale yellow spider flowers throughout the year. Leaves are dark green and oval shaped.

249. GREVILLEA 'AUSTRAFLORA COPPER CREST'

Low growing prickly shrub with attractive pink toothbrush flowers and copper coloured new growth. Flowers spring and autumn.

250. GREVILLEA BANKSI

There are two common colour forms – a red and a cream. A rapid growing large shrub to 3 m, popular in N.S.W. and Queensland. Has pale green divided foliage and large cylindrical flower spikes throughout the year. There are also some prostrate forms available. Adapts well to coastal planting.

248

251. GREVILLEA BAUERI

Variable shrub. The most popular forms are prostrate. Leaves are pale to dark green and may be wavy or markedly twisted. Flowers are red to pink and white spider flowers which may turn black with age, occurring throughout summer. Requires good drainage.

252. GREVILLEA BIPINNATIFIDA

A straggling shrub to 2 m with flowers similar to G. 'Robyn Gordon' (a hybrid produced from G.bipinnatifida).Two leaf forms are common. One form has blue rigid foliage and pale orange flowers. The second has softer green foliage and red flowers. Both forms require regular pruning to maintain good habit. Flowers throughout the year.

253. GREVILLEA BITERNATA

A prostrate grevillea with finely divided deep green foliage and fragrant white flowers. An excellent vigorous ground cover occasionally producing upright flower spikes which if not trimmed after flowering will develop into branches. Flowers in spring. Often sold as G. tridentifera.

Ph:MWH 252

251

255

253

254

256

254. GREVILLEA 'BOONGALA SPINEBILL'

A dense shrub to 2 m with deeply serrated foliage and a profusion of red toothbrush flowers over a long period in spring and summer. This hardy species is particularly favoured by birds.

255. GREVILLEA BUXIFOLIA

Small to medium shrub with dull green hairy foliage and large diameter silver-grey spider flowers held above the foliage. Flowers for long periods but requires good drainage.

256. GREVILLEA CALEYI

This medium shrub with soft hairy and deeply divided foliage features attractively purple-tinged new growth and a profusion of purple toothbrush flowers. Requires a particularly well drained site.

257. GREVILLEA 'CANBERRA GEM'

A dense medium shrub with narrow spikey foliage with numerous pink to red spider flowers. Flowers in spring. A very hardy species, popular in landscaping.

258. GREVILLEA CAPITELLATA

A varying shrub to 1 m. Leaves may be green or grey. Flowers are attractive dark red or wine coloured, hanging in pendant clusters in winter and spring. Very hardy and ideal for rockeries.

259. GREVILLEA 'CASCADE'

A vigorous tall shrub with an enormous spread – up to 5 or even 10 m. An excellent dense and prickly screen plant. White spider flowers. Performs best in a sunny site with good drainage.

260. GREVILLEA CHRYSOPHAEA

A small shrub with dull green oval leaves. Deep yellow spider flowers in winter and spring. An outstanding shrub for a well drained position.

261. GREVILLEA 'CLEARVIEW DAVID'

Vigorously growing medium shrub with bright red and cream flowers winter and spring. Particularly hardy. Showy when in flower, and popular in landscaping work. A variegated form is also available – G. 'Red Dragon'. *See photo page 36.*

257   258

Ph: MWH   264

265

266

Ph: MWH   267

265

268

262. GREVILLEA 'CLEARVIEW ROBIN'

A grey foliaged shrub to 2 m with red and cream waxy flowers in winter and spring.

263. GREVILLEA CONFERTIFOLIA

A prostrate small shrub spreading to 1 m with attractive wine coloured flowers. An excellent pot or tub specimen. Requires ample moisture and a well drained site.

264. GREVILLEA CRITHMIFOLIA

A compact spreading shrub with densely packed soft silvery green foliage and erect clusters of white flowers. A hardy species which adapts to coastal planting.

268

265. GREVILLEA 'CROSBY MORRISON'

A very hardy grey leafed grevillea growing to 1.5 m with fine foliage and dense clusters of red and cream spider flowers in spring and early summer.

266. GREVILLEA 'DARGAN HILL'

A hardy compact shrub to 2 m with short narrow grey leaves and waxy pink spider flowers throughout the year.

267. GREVILLEA DIELSIANA

A very prickly and somewhat straggling medium shrub bearing terminal tooth-brush flower heads which may be yellow, orange and red. Some colour forms are very spectacular.

268. GREVILLEA DIMORPHA

A small rounded shrub with small bright red spider flowers in autumn and spring.

269. GREVILLEA ENDLICHERANA

Small to medium shrub with fine narrow grey foliage. Carries its white flowers in erect clusters which reach well above the foliate. A hardy species.

270. GREVILLEA 'EVANS'S CORONET'

This small to medium shrub, similar to G. buxifolia, produces flowers which open pink and age to grey.

271. GREVILLEA EVANSIANA

An open small to medium shrub with deep red or burgundy spider flowers in pendulous clusters in winter and spring.

272. GREVILLEA FASCICULATA

Generally a low sprawling shrub with light green elliptical foliage and bright red flowers winter to spring.

273. GREVILLEA FLORIBUNDA

A variable often straggling shrub 1-2 m high with dull green foliage and large woolly brown and green spider flowers in winter and spring. Has been difficult to maintain in humid coastal conditions.

269

271

274

270

274. GREVILLEA 'COASTAL GLOW'

A rather open shrub to 3 m with long narrow foliage and red or burgundy toothbrush flowers in spring and summer.

273

278

279

280

276. GREVILLEA GLABELLA

A small shrub to 1 m with prickly foliage and clusters of red flowers in winter and spring.

277. GREVILLEA GLABELLA 'LARA DWARF'

A compact bush with bright red flowers.

278. GREVILLEA GLABELLA 'LIMELIGHT'

An upright shrub to 3 m with lime green flowers.

279. GREVILLEA GLABRATA

A rapid growing medium shrub with rigid blue green divided foliage and masses of open white flowers winter and spring. Requires heavy pruning for best results.

280. GREVILLEA 'HONEYCOMB' ('COOCHIN HILLS')

An upright large shrub with showy deep golden toothbrush flowers and narrow green 'fishbone' foliage. Long flowering recent introduction.

275. GREVILLEA GAUDICHAUDI

A very attractive prostrate plant with short but broad deeply lobed leaves which are often red or bronze. Toothbrush flowers are also short and broad and are bright red. An outstanding plant also suitable for baskets and often grafted to produce a weeping standard.

275

276

281

281. GREVILLEA 'HONEY GEM'

A tall shrub with finely divided light green foliage and showy yellow cylindrical flowerheads. Rapid growing, but requires some wind protection.

282. GREVILLEA 'HOOKERANA'

A medium to large spreading shrub with finely divided bright green foliage giving the plant a dense, ferny appearance. Bright crimson toothbrush flowers are popular with birds. This is a showy species and an excellent screen plant.

282

284

286

283. GREVILLEA ILICIFOLIA

A spreading small shrub with rigid pointed and lobed foliage and red toothbrush flowers. A reasonably hardy species.

Red form   Ph:MWH   288

Brown form   288

290

291

Prostrate form   292

284. GREVILLEA 'IVANHOE'

Popular tall shrub, an ideal screen plant. Has attractive ferny foliage, bronze or burgundy in new growth, and a profusion of burgundy toothbrush flowers in winter and spring. A hardy plant which responds well to pruning.

285. GREVILLEA 'JENKINSI'

An attractive small to medium shrub with fine woolly foliage and bright red flowers over a long period.

286. GREVILLEA 'JOHNSONI'

This medium to large shrub has fine green foliage giving it the appearance of a small pine. Flowers are large, red and cream spider flowers with a pearlescent appearance. Grafted forms have been more successful than others.

287. GREVILLEA JUNCIFOLIA

An open medium shrub with finely divided foliage and striking 'golden candle' flowers in spring. Best suited to areas of low humidity.

288. GREVILLEA JUNIPERINA

Many forms of this shrub are in cultivation. They range from prostrate creeping specimens to medium shrubs. Flower colours may be greenish yellow, orange or red. Foliage is usually short and narrow with a sharp point. Generally hardy, and are used extensively in landscaping.

289. GREVILLEA JUNIPERINA 'AUSTRAFLORA LUNAR LIGHT'

A striking variegated leaf form with orange pink flowers. The green leaves are edged with cream.

290. GREVILLEA JUNIPERINA 'MONLONGOLO'

Low spreading plant with apricot flowers.

291. GREVILLEA JUNIPERINA 'PINK LADY'

Very attractive small shrub with bright green foliage and showy clear pink spider flowers.

292. GREVILLEA LANIGERA

A rounded or prostrate shrub which may reach a height of 1 m. Closely packed grey foliage, and red and cream spider flowers late winter and spring. A particularly hardy species.

293. GREVILLEA LAURIFOLIA

A vigorously growing prostrate grevillea with round leaves and dark red toothbrush flowers. Flowers spring and summer.

294. GREVILLEA LAVANDULACEA

One of the most variable of the grevilleas. Many good forms are available ranging from prostrate and cascading plants to more upright shrubs growing to more than 1 m. Foliage is fine and may be grey or green. Flowers range from white through pink to red. Long flowering period. Hardy plants, but require a well drained sunny site. There are many good named varieties available.

295. GREVILLEA LINEARIFOLIA

An open shrub with narrow foliage and white or pink spider flowers. Flower most of the year. Reasonably hardy shrub, growing to 2-3 m.

296. GREVILLEA LONGIFOLIA

Similar to and often confused with G. asplenifolia, this is a rapid growing tall shrub suitable for sun or partial shade. It has burgundy toothbrush flowers most of the year. Foliage is long, narrow and deeply serrated. Both flowers and foliage are suitable for cutting.

Pinola form 294

297. GREVILLEA 'MISTY PINK'

Similar to G. Banksi, this medium shrub produces an abundance of soft pink and cream heads of flower up to 150 mm (6 inches) long. The soft grey-green foliage is deeply divided and contrasts well with the flowers. Flowers throughout the year. An excellent bird attracting species.

298. GREVILLEA 'NED KELLY'

This plant is similar to G. Robyn Gordon but the flowers open somewhat paler and deepen in colour with age through orange to red. It is reported to grow a little larger than G. Robyn Gordon and it may be a little hardier. A medium shrub flowering throughout the year.

297

295

298

299

299

303

304

306

299. GREVILLEA OBTUSIFOLIA

A small shrub or prostrate bush with attractive pale green foliage and pendulous clusters of red and cream flowers in winter and spring. A particularly hardy ground cover, very drought resistant.

300. GREVILLEA OLEOIDES

A medium shrub with bright red spider flowers in spring and summer and deep green rigid foliage with a covering of soft silvery hairs on the underside.

301. GREVILLEA 'OLYMPIC FLAME'

A compact small shrub to 1 m with fine foliage and a mass of red and cream spider flowers in spring and summer.

302. GREVILLEA 'PINK PARFAIT'

Similar to G. 'Misty Pink' but has deeper pink flowers.

303. GREVILLEA 'PINK PEARL'

A dense medium shrub to 2 m with fine prickly needle foliage and cluster of pink and white spider flowers in winter and spring. Particularly hardy species, popular with landscapers.

304. GREVILLEA 'POORINDA CONSTANCE'

A dense rounded shrub to 2 m with dark green foliage and a sprinkling of bright red flowers throughout the year. A good hedge and landscaping plant, although other species may be more showy.

305. GREVILLEA 'POORINDA ELEGANCE'

A medium rounded shrub to 2 m with glossy dark green foliage and spectacular bi-coloured flowers. The red and yellow spider flowers are carried in clusters along the branches. A light pruning allows the flowers to be seen more easily.

306. GREVILLEA 'POORINDA FIRE BIRD'

An open shrub with narrow grey-green foliage and clusters of large bright red spider flowers from winter to summer. A long flowering medium shrub popular in areas unsuitable for G. speciosa. Fertilize sparingly.

307. GREVILLEA 'POORINDA HULA'

An attractive open bush with long arching branches carrying clusters of mauve-pink spider flowers from winter through to summer. Bears narrow green leaves, and may reach a height of 1.5 m and width of 2.5 m.

308. GREVILLEA 'POORINDA LEANE'

A dense rounded medium shrub 2-3 m in height. Has glossy mid green leaves and large diameter pale apricot flower clusters. A reasonably hardy species.

309. GREVILLEA 'POORINDA QUEEN'

Similar in many respects to G. 'Poorinda Constance', although not quite as large. Orange spider flowers throughout the year. A popular landscaping shrub.

310. GREVILLEA 'POORINDA RONDEAU'

Spectacular in flower, this dense shrub growing to approximately 1.5 m is one of the most popular Poorinda hybrids. It bears a profusion of deep red spider flowers which almost obscure the foliage. An excellent and hardy landscape specimen.

308

309

311

310

312

313

Ph:MWH 313

316

Ph:MWH 317

311. GREVILLEA 'POORINDA ROYAL MANTLE'

Probably the most widely planted prostrate grevillea, 'Royal Mantle' produces a dense foliage cover which inhibits weed growth. Produces an abundance of burgundy toothbrush flowers for most of the year. Particularly vigorous grower tolerating a wide range of soil types. Fertilize sparingly.

312. GREVILLEA 'POORINDA SIGNET'

A dense spreading shrub to 1.5 m with pendulous clusters of unusual red and white flowers.

Ph:MWH 317

313. GREVILLEA PTERIDIFOLIA

An erect open shrub to 3 m with fine divided foliage and a profusion fo rich, golden toothbrush flower spikes throughout the year. An excellent bird attracting species, although somewhat frost tender. A prostrate form is also in cultivation.

314. GREVILLEA QUERCIFOLIA

Small shrub with leaves resembling the European oak. The mauve flower spikes are held above the foliage in spring. Not suited to humid conditions.

315. GREVILLEA REPENS

An open ground cover with dark green glossy holly-like foliage, bronze tinged in new growth. Wine coloured toothbrush flowers in summer.

316. GREVILLEA RIVULARIS

A very prickly grevillea which makes an ideal animal barrier and bird retreat. Although the height is usually less than 2 m, the spread may be as much as 4 m. Toothbrush floweers are an unusual pale lilac and yellow but are not conspicuous. A particularly hardy shrub, tolerant of some shade. Long flowering.

317. GREVILLEA ROBUSTA

This is the well known 'silky oak'. A large ornamental tree, often used for street planting, and occasionally used as an indoor plant when young. It is a rapid growing hardy tree, seldom reaching more than 20 m in cultivation. The pale green leaves are soft and ferny. The flowers, which are produced in abundance in late spring, are rich golden toothbrush spikes which literally drip nectar and are very attractive to birds. Equally well suited to coastal and inland plantings.

318. GREVILLEA 'ROBYN GORDON'

One of the best known grevilleas, 'Robyn Gordon' is a medium rounded shrub with fern-like foliage growing to 1.5 m. Long slender branches arch under the weight of large red cylindrical flower spikes which occur in profusion throughout the year. A spectacular shrub which responds well to annual pruning.

319. GREVILLEA ROSMARINIFOLIA

There are many forms of this very variable plant. The most common form is a dense, rounded shrub 2-3 m tall with needle like foliage and pink and white spider flowers in spring and autumn. An excellent hedge plant which may be pruned in a formal manner if desired. A cream flowered form is sold as G. rosmarinifolia 'lutea'.

320. GREVILLEA 'SANDRA GORDON'

Often erroneously considered to be a yellow flowered form of G. 'Robyn Gordon', G. 'Sandra Gordon' may attain a height of 5 m with a similar spread. Severe pruning will make this otherwise open shrub more compact. The deeply divided foliage is a dark silvery-green. Flower spikes are large, yellow, one-sided brushes. A fast growing but frost tender shrub, ideal for attracting birds.

321. GREVILLEA SERICEA

Commonly a compact long-flowering 1 m shrub. May be taller or more open in semi-shade. Small oval leaves and masses of lilac to pink spider flowers. A white flowered form is also available. A form from the Collaroy Plateau has richly coloured flowers on a more open shrub.

322. GREVILLEA SHIRESSI

A rounded hardy shrub to 3 m with large dark green leaves with prominent veins. Flowers are pale green and mauve and are borne in clusters inside the bush winter and spring. An attractive foliage shrub. May be planted in partial shade.

323. GREVILLEA 'SHIRLEY HOWIE'

A dense rounded shrub to 1.5 m with a good display of mauve spider flowers. A reliable plant for most soils.

324. GREVILLEA 'SID CADWELL'

A spreading shrub to 2 m high. The low spreading branches have dull prickly 3-lobed leaves. Fragrant red toothbrush flowers are produced in abundance throughout the year. Requires a well drained position.

325. GREVILLEA SPECIOSA
(formerly known as G. punicea)

A very showy and hardy species which may reach 2-3 m in height. Large red

318

318

319

320

spider flowers are borne in clusters or wheels. Foliage may be green or blue-grey and of varying length. Requires a well drained site in sun or semi-shade.

326. GREVILLEA THELEMANNIANA

Although upright forms of this shrub are available, the prostrate forms are more commonly encountered. The striking contrast of brilliant red toothbrush flowers against the feathery grey foliage of one prostrate form is an unforgettable sight. The green leafed form has bright green fine foliage and less showy red flowers. Both forms respond well to tip pruning. A reasonably hardy species although somewhat frost tender.

321

Ph: MWH   322

324

325

323

Grey form   326

327. GREVILLEA TRILOBA

A dense prickly shrub to 2 m. Leaves have 3 sharply pointed lobes. White fragrant flowers are borne in abundance during winter and early spring. A hardy and reliable grevillea.

328. GREVILLEA VICTORIAE

A variable shrub to 2 m with pendulous clusters of deep rusty red spider flowers in winter and spring. Relatively hardy species, well adapted to colder climates.

329. GREVILLEA 'WHITE WINGS'

A rapid growing prickly shrub to 2 m often prostrate when young. Produces an abundance of white perfumed flowers in winter and spring.

330. GREVILLEA WILSONI

A very showy shrub to 1 m with prickly divided foliage and attractive clusters of red spider flowers in spring. Not really suited for coastal plantings, but excellent inland.

331. HAKEA BAKERANA

A small round shrub about 1.5 high with pale green sharply pointed needle like foliage and large clusters of pink and cream flowers on old wood.

328

329

327

329

Ph: MWH   330

130

331

332

333

334

335

336

332. HAKEA CRISTATA

A large open shrub with attractively toothed blue green foliage and small white flowers in winter. Hardy.

333. HAKEA DACTYLOIDES

A rapid growing large shrub with attractively veined leaves and showy creamy white flowers.

334. HAKEA FRANCISIANA

A medium shrub to 3 m with broad narrow leaves and spectacular red flower spikes. Needs some wind protection.

335. HAKEA LAURINA
Pin-cushion Hakea

A large often spreading shrub with broad blue green leaves and globular flower heads in red and yellow resembling pin-cushions. A highly recommended and hardy shrub. Will not tolerate excessive fertilizer.

336. HAKEA PETIOLARIS

A tall shrub with grey green foliage and deep red globular flowers with white 'pins'. An attractive fast growing shrub flowering in autumn and winter. Very hardy.

337. HAKEA SALICIFOLIA

A dense rounded shrub or small tree, excellent for hedges and windbreaks. Has broad mid green foliage, usually tipped with bronze. The small white flowers are produced along the branches in spring. Rapid growing and very reliable. Highly recommended.

338. HAKEA SUAVEOLENS

A vigorous upright shrub to 3 m with fine pale green ferny foliage and fragrant showy white flowers in autumn and winter. Responds well to pruning.

339. HARDENBERGIA COMPTONIANA
Native Wisteria

A vigorous scrambling plant or climber with showy blue pea flowers and dark green foliage. A hardy plant for semi-shade.

340. HARDENBERGIA VIOLACEA
False Sarsparilla

As for H. comptoniana but with rich purple, white or pink flowers.

337

340

338

339

Ph: MWH   341

342

Ph: MWH   343

347

346

343. HELYCHRYSUM BRACTEATUM 'DIAMOND HEAD'

A low compact perennial less than 200 mm high with soft green foliage and bright yellow papery flowers summer to winter.

344. HELIPTERUM ROSEUM

An upright annual with soft green foliage and white, pink, yellow and bronze paper flowers, excellent for cutting and drying. Prefers full sun.

345. HEMIANDRA PUNGENS
Snake Bush

An often prostrate shrub with fine needle foliage and striking flattened tubular flowers. Sometimes difficult to maintain.

346. HIBBERTIA ASTROTRICHA

A low spreading plant with round dark green foliage and showy yellow flowers. A reasonably hardy species.

347. HIBBERTIA OBTUSIFOLIA

A common variable shrub with fleshy foliage and a good display of bright yellow flowers.

341. HELYCHRYSUM BAXTERI

A beautiful small rounded clump to 300 mm with fine grey green foliage and an impressive display of white papery flowers with yellow centres. Best in full sun. Cut back after flowering.

342. HELYCHRYSUM BRACTEATUM 'DARGAN HILL MONARCH'

A vigorous perennial to 500 mm with large soft blue green foliage and large buttercup yellow 'paper' flowers spring and summer. Full sun and good drainage desirable.

348. HIBBERTIA PEDUNCULATA

A low spreading plant which roots as it goes producing a striking display of yellow flowers. An excellent hardy species.

349. HIBBERTIA SCANDENS

A vigorous twining plant with bright green fleshy leaves and large bright yellow flowers most of the year. Resistant to salt spray. Pruning maintains compact growth.

350. HIBISCUS DIVARICATUS

An erect shrub to 2 m with large yellow flowers. Very showy and reliable.

351. HIBISCUS SPLENDENS

A rounded open shrub with soft grey green foliage and very large soft pink flowers. A reliable shrub preferring a warm well drained position.

352. HOMORANTHUS DARWINIOIDES

A low open shrub with attractive grey green foliage and pendulous yellow and red flowers. An excellent rockery shrub, attractive to birds.

Ph: CHS   350

Ph: MWH   351

353. HOMORANTHUS FLAVESCENS

A low spreading shrub to 400 mm with grey green leaves on layered branches and clusters of red and cream flowers in spring and summer. An excellent plant for foliage alone. Attractive to birds.

349

352

353

Ph: MWH   354

356

355

357

354. HYMENOSPORUM FLAVUM

A small upright tree with bright green flossy foliage and showy clusters of fragrant cream flowers which age to yellow. A reliable tree needing ample moisture. Suitable for sunny or shady areas.

355. HYPOCALYMMA ANGUSTIFOLIUM

An open rounded shrub to 1 m (but often less), with a profusion of white or pink flowers in spring. An excellent rockery plant.

356. HYPOCALYMMA CORDIFOLIUM

A small rounded shrub with stem clasping heart shaped leaves. Young stems are attractively reddened. Small white flowers in spring. A variegated form known as H. cordifolium 'Golden Veil' is common in cultivation.

357. INDIGOFERA AUSTRALIS

An open upright shrub to 2 m with blue green rounded leaves and sprays of fragrant purple pea flowers in spring. Responds well to pruning.

358. ISOPOGON ANEMONIFOLIUS
Drum Sticks

An open small shrub with attractive much divided light green foliage and showy yellow flowers. A hardy plant worth growing for the foliage alone.

359. ISOPOGON ANETHIFOLIUS

Similar to I. anemonifolius and deserving of a place in any garden.

360. ISOPOGON DUBIUS

An upright prickly shrub with showy bright pink flowers. Requires good drainage.

361. ISOTOMA AXILLARIS

An attractive rounded plant to 300 mm with soft fine green foliage and a good display of blue star-like flowers. Reproduces freely from seed. Should be watched for green caterpillars which may defoliate the plant. Prefers reasonable moisture.

362. JACKSONIA SCOPARIA

An upright shrub or small tree with pendulous fine blue green leafless branches and a profusion of small yellow pea flowers. An attractive plant for both foliage and flowers. Drought resistant.

358

359

Ph: CHS   360 ·

364

363

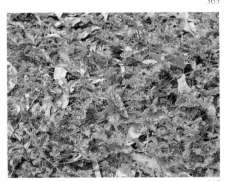

365

365

366

368

369

May be too aggressive for small areas. K. nigricans is similarl to K. rubicunda but has large and unusual yellow and black flowers.

367. *KUNZEA AMBIGUA*

A rounded shrub to 3 m with fine heath-like foliage and fluffy white flowers. A form which has mauve-pink flowers is quite showy and makes a useful screen plant. Hardy.

368. *KUNZEA BAXTERI*

A rounded shrub to 3 m with small bright green leaves and showy red bottle brush flowers tipped with gold. Requires good drainage. May be slow to flower. Attractive to birds.

369. *KUNZEA CAPITATA*

A rounded small shrub to 1 m with fine leaves and showy heads of mauve-pink flowers.

364. *KENNEDIA MICROPHYLLA*

A fine leafed mat forming plant, ideal for rockeries or hanging baskets. It spreads to 1 m and has attractive, small brick-red pea flowers. Requires good drainage.

365. *KENNEDIA PROSTRATA*
Running Postman

A prostrate spreading plant with blue-green wavy foliage and bright scarlet pea flowers.

366. *KENNEDIA RUBICUNDA*

A rampant climber with large dark green leaves and red pea flowers. Excellent soil binder and suitable for coastal planting.

363. *KENNEDIA EXIMEA*

A prostrate or trailing plant spreading to 1 m or more providing a dense cover of green foliage and bright red pea flowers.

370. KUNZEA POMIFERA
Muntries

A spreading prostrate shrub with feathery white flowers followed by berries used in jam making. Good drainage and full sun preferred.

371. KUNZEA SP. 'BADJA CARPET'

A spreading prostrate plant with much to recommend it. It has reddish stems which root at the nodes and fluffy white flowers in summer. A vigorously growing dense ground cover.

372. LAGUNARIA PATERSONI
Norfolk Island Hibiscus

A medium to large tree with rounded pale green leaves and pink hibiscus like flowers. The fruit contains numerous fine hairs which may cause skin irritation. A useful tree, resistant to salt spray.

373. LAMBERTIA FORMOSA
Mountain Devil

A rigid open shrub to 2 m with sharply pointed narrow foliage and showy orange to red flowers. Suitable for cutting. Fruits are used for decoration and doll making. Hardy.

374. LECHENAULTIA BILOBA

An open bush 300-500 mm with flowers of white or shades of blue varying to very deep blue and soft blue-green foliage. A very showy plant which may be difficult to maintain but which is worth growing even as an annual.

375. LECHENAULTIA FORMOSA

Typically a small prostrate plant, available in a wide range of colours. A brilliant red form is most spectacular and although difficult to maintain is worth growing as an annual.

376. LEPTOSPERMUM FLAVESCENS
Tantoon Tea-Tree

A rounded shrub to 3 m producing a spectacular display of white 5-petalled flowers. A reliable hardy shrub.

Kunzea SP. Ph: MWH   371

Ph: CHS   373

374

372

374

Orange form   375

378

376

In bud   377

379

377. *LEPTOSPERMUM FLAVESCENS*
'Pacific Beauty'

A very showy spreading form rarely exceeding 1 m in height.

378. *LEPTOSPERMUM LAEVIGATUM*
Coastal Tea-Tree

A dense bushy shrub or small tree with short oval or grey-green foliage and white flowers with green or red centres. A hardy shrub, tolerant of salt spray, and ideal for colonizing stabilized dunes.

379. *LEPTOSPERMUM PETERSONI*
Lemon Scented Tea-Tree

A dense rounded shrub to 3 m or more with narrow bright green foliage. Very fragrant if crushed. A good display of white flowers in spring and summer. A rapid growing and reliable screen plant benefitting greatly from regular pruning.

380. *LEPTOSPERMUM SCOPARIUM*
Tea-Tree

A variable shrub ranging from 300 mm to well over 2 m with fine pointed foliage. Many highly ornamental flowering forms and colours have been produced, predominantly in New Zealand and Canada, with names such as L.s. 'Lamberthi' and L.s. 'Damask'. These are far too numerous to be included here.

381. *LOMANDRA LONGIFOLIA*

A large tussocky plant to 1 m with long narrow strap like foliage arching to the ground with short fragrant flower spikes. This hardy plant is ideal for edges of water gardens, or as an under-storey where tree canopy makes other shrubs difficult to establish and moisture supply is reasonable.

382. *LOMATIA SILAIFOLIA*
Wild Parsley

An upright often multi-stemmed plant with much divided rigid foliage and attractive sprays of creamy white flowers. Excellent for cut flowers.

383. *LOPHOSTEMON CONFERTUS*
(syn. *Tristania conferta*)
Brush Box

A well known street or park tree with a dense canopy of mid green foliage and small white flowers. This very hardy and

Hybrid 380

useful tree will withstand heavy lopping but care should be taken not to destroy its aesthetic appeal.

MELALEUCA

Often referred to as 'paper barks', there are more than 140 species. Many, but not all, are tolerant of poorly drained soils. They range from small shrubs to tall trees and are popular garden specimens. Melaleucas have bottle brush type flowers perhaps two or three times each year. Pruning after flowering is beneficial to all Melaleucas.

384. *MELALEUCA ARMILLARIS*
Bracelet Honey Myrtle

A large rounded shrub or small tree with fine foliage and a profusion of small white bottle brush flowers. It is an excellent windbreak tree, quite hardy, and will withstand salt spray. Probably the most widely planted native.

382

384

Variegated form 383

388

385. MELALEUCA BRACTEATA

A variable species from which has been derived a number of popular cultivars. All are hardy, rapid growing and suitable for wet locations. The better known varieties are:

386. MELALEUCA BRACTEATA 'GOLDEN GEM'

This cultivar has yellow leaves and a low compact habit. It is essential to prune regularly to maintain good form. Profusion of small creamy yellow flowers.

387. MELALEUCA BRACTEATA 'REVOLUTION GREEN'

A medium shrub of compact habit with bright green foliage. Useful for a low screen. Profusion of small twisted cream flowers.

388. MELALEUCA BRACTEATA 'REVOLUTION GOLD'

Similar to 'Revolution Green' with golden yellow foliage.

389. MELALEUCA CAPITATA

A medium rounded shrub. The dark green foliage forms an excellent contrast with the globular heads of cream flowers which are borne terminally. A very hardy species.

390. MELALEUCA CUTICULARIS

Large erect shrub which makes an excellent specimen plant having attractive pale bark contrasted with light green foliage and small creamy flowers. Very hardy and tolerant of salt spray.

391. MELALEUCA DIOSMIFOLIA

Dense medium shrub with neat foliage and pale lemon flowers. A hardy foliage plant somewhat frost tender.

392. MELALEUCA ELLIPTICA
Granite Honey Myrtle

Medium shrub with small blue-grey leaves and red flowers which burst from purple spikes. A hardy and reliable species.

Ph: CHS 392

386

Ph: MWH 391

141

393. *MELALEUCA ERICIFOLIA*

Among the hardiest of all Australian plants. This is a rapid growing medium to large bushy shrub with fine green foliage bearing a profusion of white flower spikes.

394. *MELALEUCA FULGENS*
Scarlet Honey Myrtle

This rounded small shrub produces large showy flower spikes which may be orange, salmon, purple or red. It is a fine foliaged plant which demands good drainage.

395. *MELALEUCA HUEGELI*
Chenille Honey Myrtle

An upright shrub to 4 metres with attractive fine foliage and a spectacular display of cream flowers. Resistant to salt spray and adapted to most soil types.

Red form 394

396

397

396. *MELALEUCA HYPERICIFOLIA*
Hillock Bush

Large rounded shrub with 'papery' foliage. It bears bright red brushes on older wood. Requires full sun for best development but will perform well in shade if given judicious pruning. Somewhat frost tender.

397. *MELALEUCA INCANA*
Grey Honey Myrtle

An attractive medium shrub with delicate weeping foliage and cream to yellow flowers bursting from red spikes. This is a variable species; some forms are more attractive than others.

Ph: MWH 398

402

401

403

398. MELALEUCA LATERITA
Robin Red Breast Bush

A small to medium shrub. A fine foliaged species with bright red flowers on older wood. Relatively hardy.

399. MELALEUCA LEUCADENDRON

There are a number of leaf forms for this small weeping tree. Leaves vary from fine to broad, are dark green and form a good foil to the white flowers. A graceful and hardy tree.

400. MELALEUCA LINARIIFOLIA
Snow in Summer

A number of forms of this attractive plant are available. These range from small shrubs to small trees. Leaves may be light green or tinged with purple. They produce a profusion of white flowers with small white brushes which cover the plant and give rise to such names as 'Snow in Summer', 'Snowstorm' etc. Hardy and tolerant of moist conditions.

401. MELALEUCA MEGACEPHALA

Although not as reliable as some other Melaleucas, the showy deep yellow globular flower heads make this plant worth a try. Silvery-green leaves. Medium shrub.

402. MELALEUCA NEMATOPHYLLA
Wiry Honey Myrtle

This medium shrub has wiry narrow leaves. Globular flower heads are quite spectacular being mauve-pink dusted with gold and are produced terminally.

403. MELALEUCA NESOPHILA
Western Tea Myrtle

Particularly hardy species, well suited to coastal plantings. A dense shrub growing 3-6 metres with dark green leathery leaves and globular flower heads which open mauve-pink and fade to white.

Ph: CHS 402

143

404. MELALEUCA NODOSA

A particularly hardy species adapted to a wide range of soil types. Has fine needle like leaves and numerous pale yellow aromatic flowers. Large shrub.

405. MELALEUCA PULCHELLA
Claw Flower

Small shrub with grey green foliage and mauve-pink claw-like flowers.

406. MELALEUCA QUINQUENERVIA
Broad Leaved Paper Bark

This well known tree, often referred to simply as a 'paper bark' is found throughout Australia and is known by many common names. It is a large handsome tree, with broad leathery leaves and bears numerous white honey scented bottle brush flowers. Flowering may occur several times a year. Used extensively in landscaping, it is adaptable to a wide variety of soil types including waterlogged soils.

407. MELALEUCA RADULA

Medium open shrub with soft grey-green leaves and pale pink or mauve bottle brush flowers. A hardy shrub.

404

406

411

407

Ph: MWH   408

Ph: CHS   412

Ph: MWH   414

408. MELALEUCA SPATULATA

Upright small shrub producing a profusion of small mauve flowers. A hardy species preferring a well drained site.

409. MELALEUCA SQUARROSA
Scented Paper Bark

Dense, medium rounded shrub with neat foliage and showy sweetly perfumed cream flower spikes. Prefers moist conditions.

410. MELALEUCA STRIATA

A low spreading shrub bearing showy pink terminal flower spikes. Quite hardy, but prefers a well drained, sunny site.

411. MELALEUCA STYPHELIOIDES
Prickly Paper Bark

Large shrub or small tree with papery bark and small pointed leaves. Bears creamy white flowers in summer. Very hardy, suitable for poorly drained or drier sites and often used as a street tree.

412. MELALEUCA THYMIFOLIA

This small rockery shrub which produces showy violet fringed flowers and has fine narrow leaves is often found on poor soils, and will thrive on a moist site.

413. MELALEUCA WILSONI

Similar to M. thymofolia, although a little larger. Flowers are lilac to reddish pink.

414. MELASTOMA DENTICULATUM

An open shrub to 1 m or more with coarse rounded leaves and large mauve-pink flowers with yellow anthers throughout the year. A good plant for shady situations. Improved by regular pruning. Very similar to the introduced 'Tibouchina' species.

415. MELIA AZEDARACH VAR. AUSTRALASICA
White Cedar

An attractive small tree with deciduous fern like foliage, purple and white flowers and showy berries. Common in cultivation, but may be attacked by hairy caterpillars. Birds are attracted to the fruit.

416. MICROMYRTUS CILIATA

A variable small shrub with small dark green leaves and a profusion of small white flowers which redden with age. Long flowering. Requires a well drained position.

417. MYOPORUM DEBILE

A small trailing plant with white or blue star-like flowers and showy coloured berries – red, purple or green. Very adaptable.

418. MYOPORUM PARVIFOLIUM

A dense prostrate plant, spreading 1-2 m or more, rooting at the nodes, with bright green crowded foliage and masses of white star-like flowers in late spring. A pink flowered form and a purple leafed form are in cultivation.

In winter 415

419. OLEARIA PHLOGOPAPPA

An upright shrub to 1.5 m with grey-green foliage which bears showy daisy flowers in white, blue, pink or mauve. A reliable species requiring regular pruning.

420. OXYLOBIUM SCANDENS

A vigorously growing prostrate plant spreading to 3 m with deep green oval leaves and a good display of yellow pea flowers. Some forms are very hardy.

416

146

416

419

420

Ph: MWH 421

421. PANDOREA JASMINOIDES
Bower of Beauty

A vigorous climbing plant with dark green shiny foliage and clusters of large pink trumpet shaped flowers with deep red throats produced in abundance throughout the summer. Prefers moist soils and some protection.

422. PANDOREA PANDORANA
Wonga Wonga

A hardy vigorous climber with glossy green leaves and a profusion of tubular flowers which fall to carpet the ground. Flower colour varies from cream to pink with deeper coloured spotted throat.

423. PATERSONIA FRAGILIS
Native Iris

A small clump plant with strap like leaves and small iris like flowers.

424. PHEBALIUM SQUAMEUM

A bushy plant or small tree with short oval leaves and creamy yellow flowers.

425. PHEBALIUM SQUAMULOSUM

A variable shrub to 3 m with pale to rich yellow flowers.

426. PHYLA NODIFLORA

A vigorously growing matting plant which roots as it spreads and bears heads of small pink flowers. A very useful plant as a lawn substitute. Plants become smaller and more compact under heavy traffic, but spread is unaffected.

422

422

Ph: CHS   423

427. PIMELEA FERRUGINEA

A dense rounded shrub to 1 m or more with small oval glossy green leaves and a profusion of pink to deep pink terminal flower heads. Reasonably hardy. Prefers a well drained friable soil. Sunny or partly shaded position.

428. PITTOSPORUM RHOMBIFOLIUM

A small to medium tree with round glossy green leaves with dense terminal cluster of creamy white flowers followed by masses of orange berries held through autumn and winter. A good tree for warm coastal sites. Very showy during the winter months.

424

425

Ph: MWH 426

Bon petite Ph: MWH 427

428

429

429. *PITTOSPORUM UNDULATUM*

A very hardy and dense small tree with dark green shiny leaves and terminal clusters of very fragrant white flowers in spring followed by attractive orange fruit.

430. *PODOCARPUS LAWRENCEI*
Mountain Plum Pine

A variable often prostrate plant with narrow grey-green leaves and small flowers followed by attractive red fruit.

431. PODOCARPUS ELATUS
Plum Pine

A medium to large tree, often smaller in cultivation, with narrow sharp pointed foliage and bluey-black plum like edible fruit. A reliable species. Good for shade and a decorative house plant while young.

432. POMADERRIS FERRUGINEA

A bushy shrub to 3 m with leaves bearing rusty coloured hairs on the undersurface. Large sprays of bright yellow flowers cover the bush in spring. Prefers good drainage and full sun.

PROSTANTHERA

A large family of small to large shrubs with showy tubular flowers and aromatic foliage. A great many are in cultivation. Two are described, but many more make good garden specimens.

433. PROSTANTHERA LASIANTHOS
Victorian Christmas Bush

A compact medium shrub or small tree. Has sprays of white flowers with mauve throats. A rapid growing adaptable species.

434. PROSTANTHERA OVALIFOLIA
Purple Mint Bush

An upright shrub to 2 m or more with mid green aromatic foliage and a dense covering of purple tubular flowers in spring. Common in cultivation.

435. PTILOTUS OBOVATUS
Mulla Mulla

A low compact shrub with silver-grey foliage and spikes of pink and grey fluffy flowers.

436. RHAGODIA NUTANS
Salt Bush

A low spreading plant with grey foliage and small flowers followed by bright red fruit. An excellent plant for embankments, ground cover or contrast foliage. Very hardy and drought resistant.

432

433

435

Ph: MWH   437

438

434

437. RHODODENDRON LOCHAE

Showy red trumpet flowers on a low spreading shrub with bright green glossy foliage. An ideal tub plant, preferring a well composted acid soil, reasonable moisture and some shade.

438. RICINOCARPUS PINIFOLIUS
Wedding Bush

A rounded shrub to 1 m with narrow bright green foliage densely covered with white flowers in spring. Prefers a well drained soil in full sun.

439. RULINGEA HERMANIFOLIA

A low spreading often ground hugging shrub with dark green crinkly foliage and white star shaped flowers in spring. A hardy plant preferring full sun.

436

439

440. SCAEVOLA AEMULA

A vigorously growing ground cover with soft green foliage and large rich mauve-blue fan shaped flowers.

441. SCAEVOLA ALBIDA

A spreading plant to 1 m or more across with pale blue fan shaped flowers. A hardy ground cover responding well to moist soils.

442. SCAEVOLA CALENDULACEA

A dense and vigorous trailing plant with bright green succulent leaves, blue fan flowers and fleshy purple fruit. Tolerant of salt spray and good for dune stabilization.

443. SOLLYA HETEROPHYLLA
Bluebell Climber

A vigorous climbing plant with small bright green oval leaves and bluebell flowers. White and pink forms are also available. Flowers are followed by fleshy fruit. A very hardy climber which may be induced to form a dense shrub with periodic pruning.

444. SOWERBAEA JUNCEA
Vanilla Lily

A small tufted plant with blue green rush like foliage and showy heads of purple vanilla scented flowers. Ideal for moist sandy soils and small pots.

445. SPYRIDIUM CINEREUM
Dusty Miller

A low prostrate shrub with dark green oval leaves and small white flowers which give the appearance of the plant having been dusted with flour. A reliable ground cover, tolerant of reasonable shade.

446. STENOCARPUS SINUATUS
Fire Wheel Tree

A small rather slow growing tree with dense dark green foliage and showy red 'wheels' of flower. Ideal for warm moist climates.

447. STYLIDIUM GRAMINIFOLIUM
Grass Trigger Plant

A small tufted plant with grass like foliage suitable for small pots or rockeries. Pink flowers are produced on long spikes above the foliage. In a unique method of pollination, insects 'trigger' the stamen to strike the insect, depositing pollen which is carried to the next flower.

440

441

Pink flowered form   443

152

Ph: MWH 442

444

449

448. *STYPANDRA GLAUCA*

A tufted plant with long arching stems bearing rows of opposite leaves and blue flowers with prominent yellow anthers. Does best in dry shady conditions.

449. *SWAINSONA GALEGIFOLIA*

An attractive perennial to 1 m with blue green fern-like foliage and sprays of large mauve purple pea flowers. A hardy plant in sunny or semi-shaded conditions.

Ph: CHS 448

445

Ph: CHS 447

450. SYNCARPIA GLOMULIFERA
Turpentine

A dense upright tree to 20 m with dull green foliage and interesting straight grained fibrous bark. Bears small white fluffy flowers. An excellent wind break tree, being hardy and fast growing.

451. SYZYGIUM COOLMINIANUM

A small tree with shiny rounded leaves, fragrant when crushed. Showy white flowers and tasty blue fruit. Suitable for warm moist gardens.

452. SYZYGIUM LUEHMANNI

A small tree with dark glossy leaves, red or bright pink in new growth, white fluffy flowers and attractive red fruit. Very hardy and well recommended.

453. SYZYGIUM MOOREI

A medium tree with dark glossy rounded leaves and red or pink flowers followed by large edible white fruit.

454. TELOPEA SPECIOSISSIMA
N.S.W. Waratah, Waratah

A spectacular flowering shrub to 3 m. For best success in cultivation, choose well grown healthy plants, do not allow to become pot bound and provide with a well drained soil rich in humus. Fertilize regularly with a low phosphorus fertilizer. Prefer full sun. Plants may bloom from 2 years onwards and may easily carry 6-20 blooms at first flowering, increasing substantially in number with age.

455. THOMASIA MACROCARPA

A small shrub to 600 mm with cloth like serrate foliage and large pink flowers. Very showy.

456. THOMASIA PETALOCALYX

A rounded shrub to 600 mm with wrinkled foliage and attractive papery flowers which are pink with a black centre. A reliable species preferring full sun.

450

Ph: MWH 451

457. THRYPTOMENE SAXICOLA

A rounded shrub with soft arching branches bearing masses of pale pink flowers in winter and spring. Very hardy, long flowering and suitable for cut flowers.

458. THYSANOTUS MULTIFLORUS
Fringe Lily

A small tufted plant to 300 mm with deep green rush like foliage and showy clusters of mauve pink flowers with feathery petals. Prefers well drained sunny situation with ample moisture.

452

454

Ph: CHS 457

460

459. *TRISTANIOPSIS LAURINA*
(syn. Tristania laurina)

Water Gum

An attractive small tree with mid-green pointed foliage, often red tinged, and a good display of small yellow flowers. Very hardy. An excellent street tree.

460. *VIOLA BETONICIFOLIA*

Native Violet

A small tufted plant for rockeries or pots with upright stems carrying bright mauve flowers. Tolerant of dry conditions.

Ph: MWH 458

455

Ph: MWH 459

456

461

461. *VIOLA HEDERACEA*
Native Violet

An attractive and useful ground cover suitable for moist soils. Produces a dense cover of bright green foliage and erect stems with small blue and white violet flowers. A plant which roots as it spreads, and may be divided easily.

462. *WESTRINGIA BREVIFOLIA VAR. 'RALEIGHI'*
Blue Westringia

A medium rounded shrub with blue grey foliage and a good display of blue flowers for most of the year. A reliable hardy shrub requiring regular pruning for compact growth.

462

463

463. *WESTRINGIA FRUTICOSA*
Coastal Rosemary

A very hardy rounded shrub prized by landscapers for its ability to withstand harsh conditions including salt laden air. It has fine blue grey foliage and white flowers borne back to back on the upper ends of the branchlets. Flowers most of the year. An excellent hedge plant which benefits from regular pruning. A variegated form is available.

464. *WESTRINGIA GLABRA*

An upright open shrub to 1.5 m with blue grey foliage and mauve blue flowers. A very showy and hardy species, which will benefit from pruning.

Books worth reading

Adams, George Martin, *Birdscaping Your Garden*. Rigby Publishers, 1980.

Blombery, Alec. M. *Practical Gardening & Landscaping*. Angus & Robertson Publishers, Australia, 1984.

Burke, Don *Growing Grevilleas in Australia & New Zealand*. Kangaroo Press, Kenthurst, N.S.W., 1983.

Elliott, Gwen *Australian Plants for Small Gardens and Containers*. Hyland
House Publishing Pty. Limited, Melbourne, Victoria, 1979.

Society for Growing Australian Plants, *Australian Plants*. Vols. I to IX (1959-1984).

Stones, Ellis *Australian Garden Design*. The Macmillan Company of Australia Pty. Ltd., South Melbourne, 1971.

Wrigley, J.W., Fagg, M. *Australian Native Plants*, William Collins Publishers Pty. Ltd., Sydney, 1979.

Explanation of words you may not know

Annual   A plant which grows from seed, matures, flowers and dies within one year.

Bipinnate   See pinnate. Leaves are twice divided.

Bract   Modified leaf at the base of a flower.

Catkin   A spike of flowers without petals.

Cultivar   Variants which arise in cultivation, generally through hybridization, which are sufficiently interesting to be given their own name.

Form   A minor difference from the usual form of the species such as a different flower colour or growth habit.

Glabrous   Hairless, smooth.

Glaucous   Blue-green with a whitish bloom (like a cabbage).

Hybrid   Offspring of two plants of different species.

Juvenile foliage   Foliage of a young plant, later replaced by different, adult foliage.

Perennial   A plant which lives for several years.

Phyllode   A modified leaf stalk (like a spike) acting as a leaf. Common in Acacia species.

Pinnate   Compound leaf with the leaflets arranged on opposite sides, as in a feather.

Sp./Species   A name given to closely related plants within the same family, it is like a botanical 'first name'. It is unusual for plants of one species to 'breed' with those of another species.

Ssp/Subspecies   A subgroup within a species which is slightly different from others in the species and usually has a different geographical distribution.

Var.   A 'variant' which differs slightly from others in the species.

Index of common names

Numbers given in index refer to plant indentification number.